ESSENTIAL
Frank Lloyd Wright

ESSENTIAL

Frank Lloyd Wright

Caroline Knight

p

DEDICATION

TO PAUL, WHO MADE IT POSSIBLE,
AND IN LOVING MEMORY OF MY FATHER,
KENNETH LAMB, WITH WHOM I LEARNED
TO LOOK.

Front cover: The Guggenheim Museum, New York (detail)
Courtesy of Richard Bryant/Arcaid
Back cover: Beth Sholom Synagogue
Courtesy of Alan Weintraub/Arcaid

This is a Parragon Book
This edition published in 2003

Parragon
Queen Street House
4 Queen Street
Bath BA1 1HE, UK

ISBN: 1-40542-319-6

A copy of the CIP data for this book is available from the British
Library upon request.

The right of Caroline Knight to be identified as the author of
this work has been asserted in accordance with Section 77 of the
Copyright, Designs and Patents Act of 1988.

Picture research: Image Select International
With thanks to the Frank Lloyd Wright Foundation for
permission to reproduce images.

Printed and bound in China

CONTENTS

INTRODUCTION

Although we think of Frank Lloyd Wright as a thoroughly modern architect he was very much a product of the nineteenth century, having been born in Richland Center, Wisconsin, in 1867. His parents were an itinerant and dissatisfied musician–preacher, William Cary Wright, and his second wife Anna Lloyd Jones, a member of the God Almighty Joneses', a close-knit and God-fearing Welsh family who lived in Wisconsin. The influence of both of his parents appears in Wright's work: his father's love of music was formative, and even before he was born his mother had decided that he should be an architect. When he was small she gave him the Froebel gifts – geometric shapes, designed by the German educator Friedrich Froebel, founder of the Kindergarten system, which were specifically intended to help children develop their spatial and analytical understanding of the world around them.

From 1878 Wright began to spend the summers with his mother's family. He came to know the valley close to Spring Green, Wisconsin intimately, and both the area and the family who lived in it had a profound influence on him. They formed a group who faced the world united, having almost a frontier mentality, while at the same time fostering a resilient spirit of individualism. His aunts founded one of the first 'progressive' schools in the United States (for which Wright designed buildings; see the Hillside Home School, page 46). When, in later life, he faced personal turmoil it was to this valley that he returned – despite the fact that his relatives did not always approve of his increasingly flamboyant lifestyle.

After the end of his parents' marriage in 1885, Wright began to work for Allan D. Conover at the University of Wisconsin's department of engineering, where he also studied for two semesters. During this time he assisted the architect Joseph Lyman Silsbee who was designing a chapel for the Lloyd Jones family. When Wright went to Chicago in 1887 he found work in Silsbee's studio. A few months later Wright moved to the studio of Adler and Sullivan, the most avant-garde practice in Chicago at that time. Louis Sullivan's was the only influence ever acknowledged publicly by Wright, and despite their acrimonious separation six years later, Wright would go on to refer to him as his 'Lieber Meister' (beloved master).

Adler and Sullivan was a good place for Wright, not only because Sullivan appreciated just how talented his new young assistant was and gave him a large amount of leeway as a result, but also because the firm specialised in commercial work – so Wright's preoccupation with domestic buildings was given free rein. When commercial clients wanted a house built by the same firm, the commission was passed to Wright, and this is the source of his early works in Chicago.

In 1888 Wright met his first wife, Catherine Tobin, a socially polished young woman who belonged to the same Unitarian congregation. He pursued her for a year before they married and moved into his newly designed home in Oak Park, a new suburb of Chicago where he was to build a number of 'bootleg' houses over the next few years – the discovery of which would lead to the split with Sullivan. The next ten years were professionally exciting and financially successful ones for Wright, seeing not only the burgeoning of a young family – six children by 1903 – but also the growth of an excellent architectural practice, as new clients beat a path to the door of his expanding home and studio.

His great contribution during the Oak Park years was the Prairie house, which heralded a new approach to domestic architecture. Throughout his life Wright had a great capacity for reinvention and creativity, and during the 1890s he sought to define a new aesthetic for American domestic building – something home-grown, which did not refer to European models but used local materials from local sites for local clients. He used the landscape – the flat open spaces of the mid-West – and its materials – local brick and stone – to create buildings that enhanced the lives of the families who lived within them. His houses encouraged the flow of people around generous spaces (you could get in and out of almost any room by more than one doorway) but with a central gathering point, usually a fireplace. These houses offered protection from the baking heat of summer: they had overhanging eaves (the roof extending out beyond the walls) with casement windows opening just beneath them. He preferred casements, windows that open outwards on a hinge down one side, as they suit the human arm and hand so easily. Often the eaves flared far beyond the house: Wright learned the strength of steel in the shipyards of Chicago and used great metal beams to create dramatic cantilevered extensions and floating balconies that emphasised the horizontality of the Prairie houses. In addition he embraced the use of the machine in architecture and design, as a means of enhancing the beauty of natural materials by highlighting their own qualities (so wood could be cut to show its patina to best advantage, for example).

Most of his houses were built on a unit plan, with an underlying grid that made building them relatively straightforward. This habit, which became enormously significant in his later Usonian houses, began as early as the 1880s. To begin with he used units of squares or rectangles and it was not until the 1930s that the more unexpected shapes, such as diamonds, triangles and hexagons, came into his repertoire. The Prairie houses tended to be set on either a cruciform or a pinwheel plan. The cruciform is simply a cross: a horizontal and vertical axis, one larger than the other but geometrically related, symmetrical and often with a living space of three zones taking up the larger axis. The pinwheel, on the other hand, is dynamic, not static. Think of a cross with a long narrow vertical axis and a short thick horizontal one. This gives a rectangle in the middle and four segments (two fat and two thin). So swap the top narrow segment of the vertical axis with the short fat left-hand segment, and you get a pinwheel. The beauty of a pinwheel is that while it keeps a balance and proportion between the different areas of a house, it allows for definition of spaces and visual movement (narrow to wide, or enclosed to opened) between them, making the interior volumes much more interesting to inhabit. Wright was a master of this spatial manipulation.

After the Prairie houses, financial security, social recognition and professional plaudits followed. Wright had it all but it was too much – he fell in love with another woman in his social circle and caused a scandal by leaving his wife and family to travel with her to Europe. There he published his work in what is known as the *Wasmuth Portfolio* of drawings. They left in 1909, and although he tried to take up his old life again in 1910 it was no good. Wright and his new love, Mamah Borthwick Cheney, moved to his childhood valley in Wisconsin, where he built what was to be one of his life's works and greatest buildings, Taliesin.

Tragedy followed in 1914 when a crazed servant secured all of the doorways of the domestic quarters but one and then set fire to the house, waiting outside the only exit with an axe. Mamah and her children were horrifically murdered. The servant's motive is still shrouded in mystery. Wright rebuilt at once, and he continued to adapt and improve Taliesin until the end of his life – the three major relationships after his first marriage all belonged there.

After Mamah's death Wright quickly became involved with another woman, Miriam Noel, a sculptor whose mental instability was to cause him nightmares. Their marriage and eventual divorce cost him a great deal in terms of both money and emotional energy. For the rest of the decade and the early years of the 1920s he produced little work of great note apart from the first of the textile-block houses. Wright was alive to the possibilities, both economic and aesthetic, of new materials, or old materials reinterpreted in the light of new technologies, and he liked working with concrete (Unity Temple, one of his greatest buildings, was made of poured concrete). Textile blocks were decorated, reinforced concrete bricks that enabled a degree of patterning on a plain surface without visible joins. Wright made increasing use of them from the early 1920s onwards.

Wright began collecting Japanese prints quite early on in his career, having been inspired by the Japanese exhibit at the International Exhibition in Chicago in 1893. He and Catherine travelled to Japan in

1905, and this passion found a creative outlet in the great Imperial Hotel, Tokyo, and various other commissions in that country.

By the time of the 1929 Wall Street Crash and the Great Depression, Wright was in his early sixties and was generally considered to be an architectural talent whose time had come and gone. He married (for the third and last time) a talented Montenegrin woman named Olgivanna, and founded a training institution at Taliesin where apprentices could come to learn from him. His connection with Arizona also reached fruition at this time. In fact, his second great burst of creativity was to follow: over the next ten years he built a mixture of extraordinary houses, both for the luxury market and to a more restricted budget, and produced some astounding commercial designs – famous names such as Fallingwater, the Johnson Wax building and tower, the Price tower and his next contribution to domestic architecture, the Usonian house.

Wright believed that the city had become redundant in America, and that the way forward was a new tapestry of land-use, based on smaller administrative units and offering common services such as multi-faith places of worship, schools, the police and the justice system. The inhabitants would live on a 1-acre tract of land in a Usonian house – of which Wright designed large numbers in variations on the original theme. Still desirable residences today, they generally consist of one storey, with radiant heating, built on a grid for ease of construction. They are divided into two zones, one for living and one for sleeping, with the kitchen replaced by a workspace. Wright took note of social change and realised that the modern American family no longer needed a separate dining room; eating was done in a special area of the living room, close to the workspace. Materials could be cheap or expensive: board-and-batten with insulation or specially quarried stone. These houses were very private – they presented a secretive face to the outside world, but often had a whole wall of floor-to-ceiling windows (the so-called 'windowall') facing the garden.

In addition, Wright considered the problem of producing low-cost housing, and he explored the possibilities of prefabrication, working with property developers to try to bring his architecture to the attention of a broad American public. This venture was never wholly successful, as his houses always came in a bit too expensive for ordinary workers, but his contributions to the debate were decisive. In addition, he became involved in planned communities, from civic centres to a college campus and residential developments. Wright was endlessly inventive within his own unique style.

Perhaps the most famous of his designs was built near the end of his life, although it would not have taken so long had it not been so hard to find a site in New York City. The great shell-like Guggenheim Museum is itself as much of a work of art as the modern masterpieces it houses, and it is a fitting building to stand as the conclusion to this brief introduction. Wright died in Arizona in 1959 at the considerable age of ninety-one. His work continues to inspire.

FRANK LLOYD WRIGHT'S HOME, OAK PARK, ILLINOIS *1889*

Courtesy of the Frank Lloyd Wright Preservation Trust

ON 1 June 1889 Frank Lloyd Wright married Catherine Tobin. He was twenty-one, she eighteen, and they moved quickly into the house that he had designed and built for them, and which grew and expanded both spatially and architecturally for the duration of their marriage and beyond.

One of the strongest principles in Wright's architecture throughout his career was geometry – clear shapes that interlocked in a dynamic harmony. This first fully acknowledged residence's most striking external feature is the monumental shingled gable which shelters the house and covers the entrance and the bay window from the living room. On going indoors the visitor must turn at once to the left to avoid the staircase, and then emerge in the living room to face the inglenook fireplace, a common feature of early Wright houses. Wright located the hearth symbolically at the centre of the home, harking back to the days of his youth in rural Wisconsin when the fireplace was at the heart of a farming family's communal life.

Wright's architectural practice, which he opened in 1893 from this house, grew fast. He had chosen wisely in locating his family in Oak Park, a fast-growing dry suburb of Chicago that saw itself as different from the main city. He joined the tennis club, contributed to the local newspapers, competed on horseback at the Chicago Horse Show and joined the appropriate clubs. All these offered chances for him to meet potential clients, and he received many commissions.

HOUSE FOR JAMES CHARNLEY, CHICAGO, ILLINOIS *1891*

Courtesy of the John Reed Collection

THIS house, which was, astonishingly, designed when Frank Lloyd Wright was not yet 25 years old, is startlingly modern and quite unlike anything that had come before it. Frank Lloyd Wright said of the House for James Charnley that in it he first sensed the definitely decorative value of the plain surface – of the flat plane as such. What strikes the viewer more than anything about this house is the stark and highly beautiful geometry of the façade, with its polished manipulation of form and space.

The house emerges from a plinth-like lower level of ashlar stone, which contrasts pleasingly with the warm colour of the brick above. The height of the stone doubles for the central section of the house's width to include the entrance, and the windows are all recessed from the façade, without frames, so the colonnade above the doorway (see House for Rollin Furbeck page 30) is the only overtly decorative feature among the group of shapes that work together to create a satisfying whole.

Inside the house, the spatial developments are not quite as striking as those of the façade – the house is divided pretty much as its face suggests – but the staircase/atrium is skylit and lined with a characteristic Wrightian screen. The screen is beautifully carved in order to best bring out the qualities of the wood and show its texture to the greatest advantage, while extending the geometric patterning of the outside to the interior.

House for George Blossom, Chicago, Illinois *1892*

Courtesy of the Frank Lloyd Wright Foundation

THIS house, together with Wright's plans for the perspective for the Milwaukee Library competition in 1893, reveals the completeness of his grasp of the principles of classical architecture – the dominant architectural style in the United States, in the form of colonial revival, at this time. Wright abandoned classical monumentality because he believed that what was needed was a local architecture, particular to the area in which his buildings were erected and making the most of local materials. However, before he did so he created this polished example in Chicago, designed while Wright was still working for Adler and Sullivan.

The floor plan is basically cruciform, with rooms tucked into the corners, but it is slightly asymetric, giving a movement to the house that is developed in later buildings. One arm of the cruciform has the stairwell in it, and another has the fireplace, and the living room is placed along the axis with the stairwell so that the former is off-centre. As with Wright's later work, he created a flow of movement within the building so that spaces run into each other, rather as they did at his home in Oak Park. The façade is satisfying because the geometry is precise and Wright used the contrast of white trim and wood siding to give vertical and horizontal emphasis respectively. As with the Charnley house (see page 16) the ground-floor windows rest on the base block, and the central third of the façade on each side is recessed so that the corners give the illusion of being towers.

HOUSE FOR ROBERT EMMOND, LA GRANGE, ILLINOIS *1892*

Courtesy of William Allin Storrer (S.015)

WHEN Wright was moonlighting to pay for his house and maintain his increasingly comfortable lifestyle, as well as that of his wife, his mother and his two sisters, all of whom were dependent on him financially, he built three houses on a basic square plan. Like this, the other two (for Thomas H. Gale and Robert P. Parker) were built of clapboard, and the square was enlivened with octagonal towers on the reception and dining rooms. The main entrance, typically at this time, leads in three directions: into the reception room, or up the stairs, or through doors into the kitchen and utility area.

All three houses were built so as not to face the street, although their entrances open off the road. Wright did not use arches over the windows at first, preferring a rectilinear approach, but he modified this for the windows on the plan. These are solid houses and they made up the bread-and-butter work that formed the staple of his early career before the excitements and innovations of the Prairie stage.

HOUSE AND STABLES FOR WILLIAM H. WINSLOW, RIVER FOREST, ILLINOIS *1894*

Courtesy of Alan Weintraub/Arcaid

FRANK Lloyd Wright claimed this as his earliest independent commission, and it was certainly his first major one ($20,000) after he left the offices of his mentor Louis Sullivan. In it there is an early suggestion of the major distinction the architect made in his later works between public and private – the outer face of a building on to the street and the inner façade with more windows, light and increased access. Again the hearth is at the core of the building (see Frank Lloyd Wright home, page 14), easily seen from the formal rectangular entrance but separated from it by an elegant arcade of slim columns. The house is characteristically anchored to the earth by its long shape and low, hipped roof with overhanging eaves, but unusually the architect chose sash windows rather than casements.

As in his own house, Wright created a home in which the spaces flow into and from each other; the family or visitors could pass around the whole ground floor from one room to the next, through doorways that were invitingly wide.

House for Nathan G. Moore, Oak Park, Illinois *1895 & 1923*

Courtesy of Alan Weintraub / Arcaid

THIS is an unusual building for Wright in that it takes its inspiration directly from another style – English Elizabethan (sixteenth century). The pastiche is thoroughly carried out apart from the porch, which is inconsistent with the English style. The house was remodelled in 1923 after a major fire, and the ways in which the architect altered the house's exterior are interesting because, though relatively minor in themselves – new windows, loss of Tudor-y detail – they gave the house a very different look and feel. This new look is much less derivative and more typical of what might be thought of as 'Wrightian'. The picture here is of the house after the remodelling.

Originally the gables were beamed, with black beams on a white ground and decorative details in the same colour scheme giving a horizontal emphasis. After the fire these horizontal motifs were not replaced, and the gables were lengthened down to the first floor lintel line, making the appearance of the house much more dramatic and interesting, and perhaps showing the influence of Japanese design on Wright's work (see Jiyu Gakuen School, page 114). On the southerly aspect of the house, the first- and second-floor windows were visually joined into a single casement, emphasising the vertical movement of the gables, and the roof of the porch was converted into a balcony. The new façade looks fully integrated and unlike anything other than itself.

ROMEO AND JULIET WINDMILL TOWER, SPRING GREEN, WISCONSIN *1896 & 1938*

Courtesy of the Frank Lloyd Wright Foundation

THIS delightful windmill tower is composed of a diamond penetrating an octagon – symbolising Romeo and Juliet together, joining with and supporting each other. These forms are classics from Wright's Froebel training, the child education scheme that Wright's mother put him through. Invented by Friedrich Froebel, the system aims to promote self-learning by encouraging the development of the child's spatial and geometric awareness through the 'gifts'. These 'gifts' are shapes given to children in a particular order to enable them to develop both an appreciation of the geometric forms that underlie everything in nature, as well as an analytical habit of mind. The success of the system depends on the curiosity and interest of the individual child. It seems to have been a particularly sympathetic form of visual and structural education for the boy whom his mother Anna had already decided, before he was born, would be an architect.

In the Romeo and Juliet windmill tower Wright made use of techniques that he would later integrate into the structures of many of his high-rise buildings, such as the Price Tower for H. C. Price Company (see page 212). The octagon is held up by 4-by-4-inch posts at each corner, which were supported by steel struts sunk into the stone foundations. It was covered with wood shingles and horizontal board battening, which were not load bearing. These posts, and the one that supported the diamond shape from the middle, were referred to by Wright himself as influences on his later high-rise projects.

HOUSE FOR GEORGE FURBECK, OAK PARK, ILLINOIS *1897*

Courtesy of the Frank Lloyd Wright Foundation

THIS and the house for Rollin Furbeck (see page 30) were wedding gifts to his sons from Warren Furbeck, both commissioned from Wright in 1897. This house is full of geometric pattern and proportion, with the octagonal towers on either side of the porch having a diameter equal to the radius of the octagonal living room. Next to the living room is the dining room, which has an alcove along one side of it. The ends of this alcove are half-octagons, this time half rather than double the size of the towers. As so often happens in Wright's domestic architecture, the utility areas – the kitchen, laundry and pantry – are at the end of the house, and one side of the first floor is a long hall so that servants could pass from the front door to the working area without interrupting the family in the living rooms. Wright was designing this house for a family that would have had servants and there is as yet no hint of the architectural transitions of the twentieth century: the fundamental change from a 'kitchen' in the servants' area to a 'workspace' at the heart of the home.

HOUSE FOR ROLLIN FURBECK, OAK PARK, ILLINOIS *1897*

Courtesy of the Frank Lloyd Wright Foundation

THIS house was a wedding gift to Rollin Furbeck from his father, and it is interesting not only in itself, with the impressive geometric mass that it presents to the street, but also as a transitional building in Wright's development. In it he uses the cantilevered extension, a pervasive feature of his later work (see House for Frederick C. Robie, page 74), for the first time, and he departs from the simple squares and rectangles of so much of his earlier work. The floorplan is asymmetric, with extensions from the central square jutting out at different levels, for example the cantilevered balcony of the third-floor bedroom. Wright tended not to build housing to a height of more than two storeys, so this building is unusual, although he did build other three-storey houses during this period. Although it still has decorative features that Wright would soon abandon, such as the pillars with leafy capitals, it is still unmistakably the work of the master. The overhanging eaves and the raising of the ground-floor brickwork to the window sills of the second floor make the second-floor windows look hidden and discreet. In addition, this is the first time that the architect used picture windows in a domestic setting.

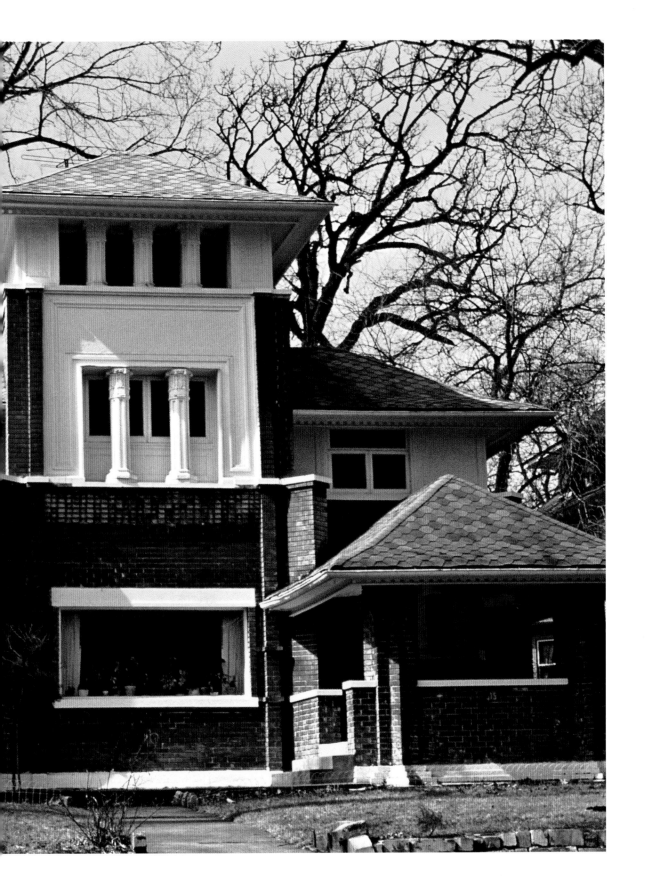

SUMMER COTTAGE FOR E. H. PITKIN, SAPPER ISLAND, DESBARATS, ONTARIO, CANADA *1900*

Courtesy of the Frank Lloyd Wright Foundation

'ALL the buildings I have ever built, large and small, are fabricated upon a unit system – as the pile of a rug is stitched into the warp.' As the architect matured, he based his works more and more upon a unit system – initially square units, but later triangles, hexagons, parallelograms – geometric shapes that form the grid on which the building is planned and fits, and that give his works part of their visual completeness.

The cottage that Wright created for E. H. Pitkin on the shores of one of the Great Lakes in Canada is an early example of this, being based upon a 4-foot unit system. The design is reminiscent both of Swiss chalets and, in its characteristic overhanging eaves, of the Japanese influence that Wright integrated into his work. From early in his career he was fascinated by Japanese prints and the aesthetics he found in them. He first saw a constructed Japanese building at the 1893 Exposition in Chicago and in 1905 he visited Japan with his wife and some of his clients. Frank Lloyd Wright's relationship with Japan and its art was to be an enduring one.

RESIDENCE FOR FRED B. JONES, LAKE DELAVAN, WISCONSIN *1900–1901*

Courtesy of William Allin Storrer (S.083)

THIS, one of the largest of Frank Lloyd Wright's building-complexes on Lake Delavan, is made up of a number of elements: a house, a gate lodge with water tower and greenhouse, and a boathouse. A bachelor who lived in Oak Park, Fred Jones used his summer house to entertain his employees at the Westlake Company of Chicago, where he was vice-president.

One of the long sides of the large rectangular living room faces the lake front, and that side and the ends are bounded by a covered porch. Two-fifths of the other long side are taken up with the fireplace, which backs on to the fireplace in the dining room – on entering the house the visitor can walk up the stairs to a gallery that looks over both rooms. Wright often made extensive use of galleries, and they occur again and again in his later Usonian works as well as in earlier houses such as the studio in his own house in Oak Park (see page 14). The gables are deeper at the top of the roof, in characteristic Japanese style.

HOUSE FOR WARD W. WILLITTS, HIGHLAND PARK, ILLINOIS *1901*

Courtesy of Alan Weintraub / Arcaid

BY the end of the century, Frank Lloyd Wright was struggling towards a new architecture. Buildings of the 1890s such as the Winslow and Charnley houses point the way but it was not until 1901 and the Willitt's house that his new ideas gain full realisation. Many architects in the United States at this time were still taking their inspiration either from classical architecture or from European styles. However, Wright was determined that there should be an indigenous style that reflected the surroundings of buildings and their purpose – their human scale as places for humans to live, in a landscape that the architect acknowledged and integrated into his design. 'The house began to associate with the ground ... and became natural to its prairie site.' Because of the harsh winters and baking summers, protection from the elements was vital, so the characteristic overhanging shallow roofs were the most appropriate. In two articles in the *Ladies Home Journal* in 1901 Wright expressed these goals, and commissions followed in generous numbers.

These and many other Prairie-house features are clear in this building. Its walls seem to rise straight from the earth – Wright was not enthusiastic about cellars – and a sense of movement is created from the first by the positioning of the entrance to the right of the main façade. The visitor therefore sees the house from the street and then has to walk around the side of it to a sequence of open and tight spaces: the spacious porte-cochère, the enclosed entry, the airy stairwell and then the short stairway bordered by wood screens, beams and panels. Only then does the visitor reach the large living room, which was the first room seen from the street and which opens on to the lot through long windows. These windows give the room a feeling of great spaciousness and anticipate later two-storey rooms in Usonian houses with floor-to-ceiling windows.

HOUSE FOR F. B. HENDERSON, ELMHURST, ILLINOIS *1901*

Courtesy of the Frank Lloyd Wright Foundation

ANOTHER feature of the Prairie houses which Wright himself emphasised is the unity of the main floor area, although it may be zoned so that different parts of the space are used for different purposes. Here, the living room, with the usual central fireplace, has alcoves at each end, one for dining and one for the owner's library, but all three spaces are united across the length of the house. This gives a greater openness and sense of space while promoting freedom of movement from one area to the next. The kitchen and the stairs are still neatly tucked away, with the bedrooms above. He also splits the flue of the living room fireplace so that the two front bedrooms each have a fireplace of their own, a device that he used again in the Stewart house (see page 90). The roof is hipped and so the house seems securely anchored to the ground, and the impression of shelter is intensified by the small windows that sit just below the roofline. Wright has used many different multiples and orientations of a single unit, which gives the façade a sense of geometric rhythm and movement.

HOUSE FOR WILLIAM FRICKE, OAK PARK, ILLINOIS

1901, additions Emma Martin 1907

Courtesy of Alan Weintraub / Arcaid

ALTHOUGH from 1900 onwards Wright was generally building more and more horizontally, this house in Oak Park is an exception in its strong verticality, reminiscent of the Rollin Furbeck house (see page 30). Unlike the tower in that building, which was only a finished attic, this tower houses a splendid billiard room.

Wright uses a combination of wood and stucco (plaster) to define and decorate the inside spaces, either on the walls or in the form of wood screens, either between rooms or around staircases. Here there is little evidence of wood on the outside and in that sense it looks forward to one of the architect's greatest works, the Unity Temple in Oak Park (see page 56). The definition of the end of the first floor and the beginning of the second at the level of the second-floor sills gives the house a typical Prairie sheltered appearance, to which the hipped roof also contributes. Its present owner, who has lived in it for thirty years, says that it is a delight for its wonderful design – he is still discovering new features.

HOUSE FOR SUSAN LAWRENCE DANA, SPRINGFIELD, ILLINOIS *1902*

Courtesy of the Frank Lloyd Wright Foundation

PRAIRIE houses tend to be either 'cruciform' (cross-shaped) or 'pinwheel' (centred on the fireplace but moving around it, with each room – reception/stairwell, living, dining and kitchen – connected via the inside corners). These fundamental patterns occur again and again in Wright's work and later, more abstract designs stand on their shoulders.

The Dana house in Springfield is a pinwheel formation around the fireplace, and is a particularly interesting one because the house was a renovation and addition rather than a new build.

Susan Lawrence Dana was widowed in 1900 and her father died in 1902 so she decided to have the family home re-created, by Frank Lloyd Wright. The architect did not demolish the old house but its lineaments are hard to trace in the new face – one of the finest of the Prairie houses. Both the living and dining rooms are two storeys high. Wright believed that to create a harmonious and unified space the architect must be intimately involved with the design not only of the bricks and mortar, wood and stone, but also of furniture, glass, lighting and soft furnishings (see House for Frederick C. Robie page 74). The decorative elements in the Dana house are inspired by the prairie outside – the shrubs and cacti as well as the yellow stone and the heat.

HOUSE FOR ARTHUR HEURTLEY, OAK PARK, ILLINOIS *1902*

Courtesy of Alan Weintraub / Arcaid

THIS solid, rectangular house shows many of the characteristic Prairie features; overhanging eaves, with windows tucked up underneath, the ground-floor walls running right up to the sills of the first-floor windows, and the sense of the building being anchored to the ground are very familiar (see House for Ward W. Willitts page 36). However, unlike other Prairie houses, and indeed unlike most of Wright's later domestic work, the rooms of the house are contained within a simple rectangular floorplan which nonetheless allows for a rotating movement and interconnection, particularly on the first (main living) floor. The façade looks monolithic, almost forbidding, in its strength and stoniness, though in fact the ground floor is well lit with windows from the sheltered loggia and the side, giving light to the large playroom that takes up about a quarter of the floor space. The upper floor is illuminated by art glass windows most of the way around. To give the outside its banded appearance, Wright specified alternating courses of different-coloured brick, set slightly forwards or slightly back, which convey a strong horizontal rhythm. The red bricks the architect used give the house a very warm and inviting appearance.

HILLSIDE HOME SCHOOL, SPRING GREEN, WISCONSIN *1902*

Courtesy of ESTO

WRIGHT first built a school for his aunts, Ellen and Jane Lloyd Jones, in 1887. During the upheavals of Wright's childhood, the Lloyd Jones family provided not only support for his mother Anna but also a strong sense of security and hearth to her children, motivating Wright to change his middle name when he was eighteen from Lincoln to Lloyd. It was to their area of Wisconsin that he returned to live with his mistress after the breakdown of his first marriage.

The sisters ran a progressive, co-educational boarding school that took children aged from five to eighteen. This new, second building housed the school's classrooms, assembly room and gymnasium, as well as the skylit physics laboratory and art room. These latter were housed in an extension to the rear, connected to it by a first-floor gallery over the school's drive.

The main part of the construction is made up of two cruciform parts of unequal height, the assembly room and the gym, connected by the passageway with classrooms and the principal's office along it. The assembly room is three storeys high, with mullioned windows from top to bottom. Unusually, Wright used these mullions as load-bearers for the cantilevered roof. At the second-floor level the assembly room has a balcony, which housed the library, and which architecturally speaking looks forward to the arrangement of the Unity Temple. For building materials the architect chose pink sandstone, oak beams and a red-tiled roof, characteristic of other buildings he created in this area. This image shows the school buildings after Wright remodelled them for the Taliesin Fellowship – see page 128.

HOUSE FOR GEORGE BARTON, BUFFALO, NEW YORK *1903*

Courtesy of the Frank Lloyd Wright Foundation

GEORGE Barton was married to Della Martin, sister of Darwin D. Martin (see page 54) and they built their house at the northern end of Della's brother's lot.

The basic floorplan of this house is a standard cruciform, with the dining room, living space and library taking up the central axis in a plan that is reminiscent of the Henderson house. Unlike in the Henderson house, the fireplace is set off-centre, in one of the inner corners of the cruciform shape, so that it warms the living-room space and the library. None of the areas is walled off from its neighbours, giving an open-plan feeling, although Wright used piers and beams below ceiling height to define the spaces. This device creates a rhythmic division, with the larger spaces (dining room and library) on the outside framing the smaller inner (living) space in a way that is not suggested by the external appearance of the house. The kitchen is tucked away behind the main stairway at the other end of the house from the entry and porch.

HOUSE FOR EDWIN H. CHENEY, OAK PARK, ILLINOIS 1903

Courtesy of the Frank Lloyd Wright Foundation

DESPITE its ground-hugging appearance, this house actually has two storeys, a basement – in which Wright wished to build a two-car garage, only to be vetoed by Oak Park city council, which feared a fire risk – and the ground floor. This held the living space – in three parts, like the Barton house – placed in front of the bedrooms at the back in a layout that looks towards the quiet zone of the Usonian houses. The fireplace is at the house's centre, with a light-well next to the flue bringing light into the house's core. The living room stretches away from it, making the centrepiece of a cross with the other living areas on each side, so there is strong movement in both directions. Again, these spaces are defined by piers and beams.

Wright designed art glass for all of the 52 windows at the main level, along with light fittings adapted to run on either gas or electricity. In addition he concealed the radiators and designed a characteristic built-in sideboard.

Although the house is remarkable for its architecture it is also notorious for being the marital home of Wright's next love, Mamah Borthwick Cheney, with whom he became involved later in the decade. The Wrights and the Cheneys socialised, and the affair apparently grew until it could be resisted no longer. Looking forward, in 1909 they left together for Germany and the next phase of Wright's creative life.

LARKIN COMPANY
ADMINISTRATION BUILDING,
BUFFALO, NEW YORK
(DEMOLISHED) *1903*

Courtesy of the Frank Lloyd Wright Foundation

THIS enormous office block was revolutionary; from the first all-glass entrance doors in the world to the placing of the company executives on the ground floor rather than the top floor, from the central light court that illuminated the offices of everyone from senior management to clerical assistant, to the company restaurant where the tables had posts at the ends so nobody could be at their heads, from the first installation of air conditioning in an office building to the first double-glazed windows for insulation of both temperature and sound, this amazing place housed 1,800 workers who processed over 5,000 letters per day. The Larkin philosophy was one of equity and improvement, and in the annex was a branch of Buffalo public library as well as a classroom. Inspirational speakers were invited to talk to the workers and encouraging aphorisms were written on the sides of the light well.

The external mass of the building is of two cubes, and the office floors were each 16 feet high and 32 feet deep. Each floor was lit by external windows set 7 feet 6 inches up on the walls, with built-in filing beneath them, and by the light from the central space that flooded in over 3-feet high internal walls. In addition, the services were all placed in the free-standing columns around the edge of the block. It is a great loss to architecture that the building was demolished in 1950 and the space is now derelict.

HOUSE FOR DARWIN D. MARTIN, BUFFALO, NEW YORK *1904*

Courtesy of William Allin Storrer (S.100)

DARWIN D. Martin was a lifelong friend of Wright's, and it was he who introduced the Larkin Company to the architect's work. This is one of the largest of the Prairie houses, and also one of the most successful. The site embraces not only the main house but also the George Barton house (see page 48) on a corner of the plot, a garage, a conservatory and a thoroughly specified gardening scheme. This included a 'floricycle', a semi-circular planting that bloomed from the early spring until the autumn.

The floorplan of the main house is symmetrical around an axis that runs from the middle of the terrace through the living room, the central fireplace and between the kitchen and reception rooms. The basic shape is a cruciform, with the dining room and library coming off the living room articulated by beams and piers in a design similar to those of other Prairie houses (see House for Susan Lawrence Dana, page 42). The whole has a symmetry and harmony that is thoroughly successful; Wright kept the floorplan displayed in his office for the next half-century. Wright also designed all the furniture and Orlando Giannini, with whom he often worked, designed the glass.

UNITY TEMPLE, OAK PARK, ILLINOIS *1905*

Courtesy of Alan Weintraub / Arcaid

WHEN the Oak Park universalist chapel burned down in the summer of 1905, the pastor (expecting a white church with a spire of the type common in New England) commissioned Wright, a local supporter, to design a new building. Instead, Wright centred his design on the idea that God's presence is in the praying congregation itself: the focus of the building was the assembly hall. He chose the square as the underlying form, both for its nobility and, alongside the material – exposed concrete, the first public building in America to be built of this fabric – for its economy. 'The wooden . . . molds in which concrete buildings must at that time be cast were always the chief item of expense, so to repeat the use of a single form as often as possible was necessary . . . this, reduced to simplest forms, meant a building square in plan,' he said.

Like the Larkin building (see page 52), the temple has a monolithic exterior – as so often, the windows are close to the roof – that belies the light flooding the interior from a combination of skylights and clerestory windows coloured amber; it always appears to be warm outside, whatever the weather. The worshipper has to walk around the building at street level to reach the entranceway, which is characteristically close and dim, before reaching the cloister around the main hall and then finally ascending the stairs to arrive in the body of the church. There are balconies around the sides to offer more seating and also to use some of the upper space afforded by the cubic structure.

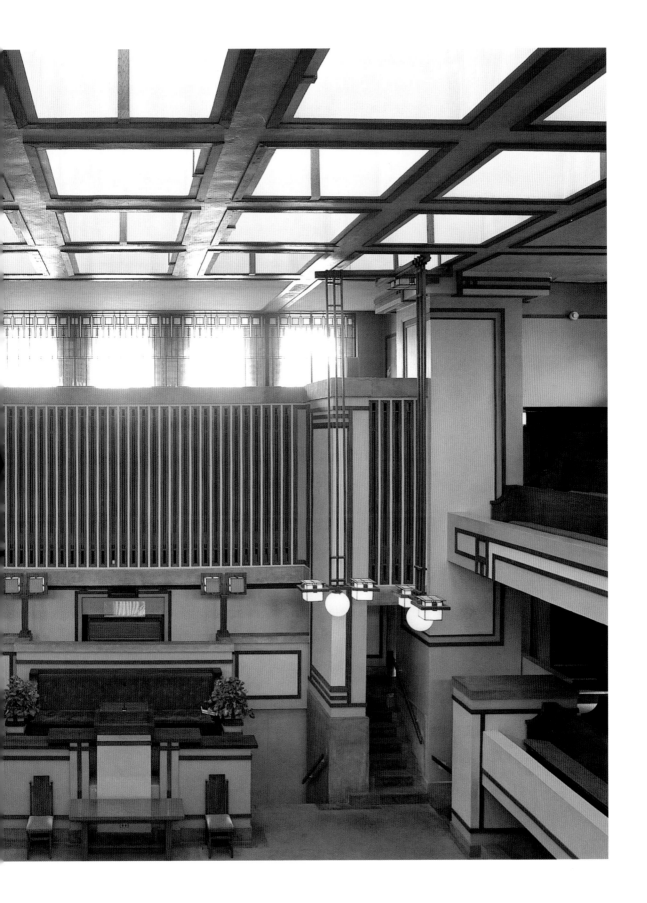

HOUSE FOR W. A. GLASNER, GLENCOE, ILLINOIS *1905*

Courtesy of Alan Weintraub / Arcaid

THE Glasner house has a dramatic location. It is perched next to a ravine that Wright originally planned to bridge, although the extension was never built; the architect often found inspiration in steep sites such as these, the most famous example of this being the much later Fallingwater (see page 134). There are two octagonal areas: the library, which grows from the living room and leads out on to a terrace above the ravine itself, and a smaller-scale sewing room, which opens from the master bedroom. The exterior was specified to be made from rough sawn wood, a finish (or lack of it) that the architect cherished in the way that he fostered rough stone in his later work. The materials were able to show their organic natures better when they were not so refined, and Wright was notorious for his preference for materials to be presented in a way that revealed them rather than dressed them up as something different.

The house has a basement but all of the main elements are sited on the ground floor. Coloured art glass was used to give decoration as well as light. The fireplace is not at the centre of the house, and this, together with the connecting corridor, looks forward to the one-storey Usonian houses that follow in the 1930s and 1940s.

HOUSE FOR THOMAS P. HARDY, RACINE, WISCONSIN *1905*

Courtesy of the Frank Lloyd Wright Foundation

THE spatial limitations of the site for this house for Thomas P. Hardy, which is situated on the banks of Lake Michigan in Wisconsin, were considered by Wright to be a special opportunity, rather than a hindrance. From the street side the Hardy House appears to occupy only one storey, but this is deceptive. In fact it drops away down the lakeside to two further levels.

Wright took the tripartite living space, as he did in the House for George Barton (see page 48), and turned it through 90 degrees so that the rooms ran from top to bottom of the house rather than along the horizontal plane of the ground. Shaping the house in this way meant that all three of the living areas have marvellous views of the lake. The main living room is two storeys deep, with the library area on the balcony and one wall of glass – strikingly modern, open and beautiful. The house's five bedrooms flank each level apart from the lowest one, where there is a bedroom on one side and the kitchen on the other.

HOUSE FOR WILLIAM R. HEATH, BUFFALO, NEW YORK *1905*

Courtesy of the Frank Lloyd Wright Foundation

WILLIAM Heath was an attorney who worked for the Larkin Company (see page 52) and his wife was the sister of one of the company's founders. It was through the remarkable administration building that Wright built for the firm that William Heath came to hear of the architect's work.

The house that Wright created for William Heath is a resolved and beautiful example of a house in the Prairie style, built of redbrick, like the Robie house. It also shares several similarities with the House for Meyer May (see page 88). Wright drew inspiration for his design solutions for both this and the Robie House in the following ways: the playroom is set down on the ground-floor/basement half level and it is lit from a well. Unfortunately the Heath House is no longer intact in the way in which it was designed by Wright: the servants' quarters are being used for other purposes, and a garage has been added, which was not on the original plans.

BANK FOR FRANK L. SMITH, DWIGHT, ILLINOIS *1905*

Courtesy of the Frank Lloyd Wright Foundation

BECAUSE this building has been substantially altered over the years it is today quite difficult to recognise anything in the building that is obviously Wrightian in character. Nevertheless, a few key features do stand out. The ahslar stone exterior, for example, seems to refer forward stylistically to the approach Wright would adopt for the desert rubble masonry of Taliesin West (see page 146), although the ahslar stone is not irregular in the way that rubble masonry is.

The monumental exterior of the Bank for Frank L. Smith certainly gives an impression of solidity and security and as such it is an entirely appropriate building for a bank. The interior is lit by clerestorey windows all the way around – that is, the roof is raised (the building is one-and-a-half storeys high) and there is a narrow band of glass just beneath it that projects diffused light into the depths of the building.

HOUSE FOR K. C. DeRHODES, SOUTH BEND, INDIANA *1906*

Courtesy of the Frank Lloyd Wright Foundation

THE ground plan of this house is symmetrical around two axes, although the servant's room on the north-west corner is an exception to this. The entryway is itself a small cruciform, with closets and flower pots filling the corner spaces, and then steps lead up into the main living area. On the visitor's left is the living room with the fireplace, and on the right is the dining room, identical in proportion. The kitchen is located behind the staircase ahead and is of similar size to the entrance area. Both living and dining rooms have terraces. Upstairs there are five bedrooms, lavishly provided with two bathrooms, unlike the Hardy residence (see page 60), which has only one for the same number. Lighting on the ground floor is from casement windows that run in a band around the front of the house, under the eaves of the porch and along the walls of the main building, but the windows upstairs are positioned directly under the eaves, below the embracing roof.

HOUSE FOR E. R. HILLS (HILLS–DE CARO), OAK PARK, ILLINOIS *1906*

Courtesy of Alan Weintraub/Arcaid

LIKE the house for Susan Lawrence Dana (see page 42), this project was not a new build for Frank Lloyd Wright. In 1883 a two-storey Victorian house was built for Frank S. Gray, who sold it to Nathan Moore in 1900. It was this house that was relocated and re-created by Wright who redesigned it in 1900, although problems prevented building from taking place until 1906. Moore gave the new building to his daughter Mary and her husband E. R. Hills as a wedding present.

The floorplan is a pinwheel, with a generous hallway at the heart of the building from which the living room, dining room and family room open. Wright designed a built-in sideboard for the dining room, and on the staircase he put a large bay window that gave Mary Hills a view of her father's house nearby. The eaves extend out from the walls to give a sense of shelter but the roof is more steeply pitched than on mature Prairie homes, so the sense of horizontal rootedness is less striking than in other houses of this period.

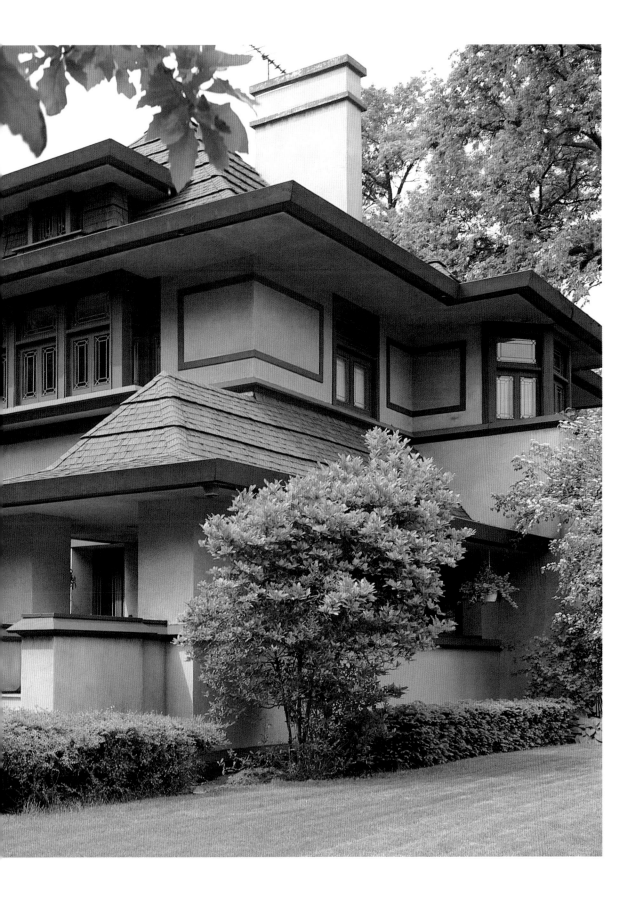

WILLIAM H. PETTIT MORTUARY CHAPEL, BELVIDERE, ILLINOIS *1906*

Courtesy of the Frank Lloyd Wright Foundation

EMMA Glasner Pettit, the sister of W. A. Glasner (see page 58), commissioned Frank Lloyd Wright to build this memorial to her husband William seven years after his death. The chapel looks much like a Prairie house from the outside, with its familiar overhanging roof, with a shallow pitch designed to hold snow rather than shed it (the insulating effects of snow were greatly valued by Frank Lloyd Wright). Its windows are tucked up close beneath to allow for some respite from the baking sun in the hot Illinois summers.

The floorplan of the chapel is T-shaped, and the large central room has a fireplace so the congregation could be kept warm during memorial gatherings. The walls are made from lime-based stucco and the trim is cypress wood on the outside and yellow pine in the chapel itself. The graves of the Pettit family are located outside the chapel; Mrs Pettit herself died in 1924.

RIVER FOREST TENNIS CLUB, RIVER FOREST, ILLINOIS *1906*

Courtesy of the Frank Lloyd Wright Foundation

Wright was one of three architect-members of this tennis club, and he collaborated with the others (Charles E. White and Vernon S. Watson) on the design of the new clubhouse in 1906. Half of the long, ground-hugging building was taken up with a hall, with fireplaces on three sides and glass windows out towards the tennis courts on the fourth. Dressing rooms, for men behind one end of the hall and women behind the other, formed the rest of the building. In the dressing rooms Wright put the windows near the roof for a combination of light and privacy.

Wright also designed the RFTC logo that appears on the wall behind the central fireplace. The interlacing of the letters is graphic and reminiscent not only of the visual effect of the net of a tennis court but also of Japanese pictograms; Wright had been collecting Japanese prints for some years and was inspired by Japanese architecture (see Summer cottage for E. H. Pitkin, page 32).

HOUSE FOR FREDERICK C. ROBIE, CHICAGO, ILLINOIS *1907*

Courtesy of Alan Weintraub/Arcaid

THE finest realisation of the Prairie house idea, and one of the most beautiful of Wright's buildings, Frederick C. Robie said of the house, 'I think it's the most ideal place in the world.'

The Robies were a well-to-do family who came to Wright because when they told other architects what they wanted, the response was 'You want one of those damn Wright houses.' In this creation Wright shows an absolute mastery over technique and environment: for example, at midsummer the sun's light just touches the bottom of the south-facing windows, thanks to the shade given by the cantilevered overhangs, but in the spring and autumn light floods in to warm the house. He used cantilevers – technology he mastered from the shipyards of Chicago – to stunning visual effect both in the terrace overhangs and in the floating brick balcony, lined and supported by another steel beam. The combination of brick, yellow mortar, art glass, wood and his own designed furniture makes for an aesthetic feast of mellow colour and harmonious proportion that is deeply satisfying. Interior spaces are defined yet flow into one another. The living room and dining room are separated by a fireplace that is open to the ceiling above the mantelpiece thanks to a double flue, and he used the familiar mechanisms of screens, piers and beams on the ceiling to guide the eye into understanding the spaces he had created.

HOUSE FOR AVERY COONLEY, RIVERSIDE, ILLINOIS *1907*

Courtesy of Alan Weintraub / Arcaid

WRIGHT himself regarded the complex of buildings for Avery Coonley as his greatest achievement of this period. It is the first house that is explicitly zoned, and the ground plan of the main buildings is two pinwheel cruciforms, joining at the tips of their long axes, one for living and one for sleeping. The complex is built around a courtyard, although unlike most buildings of this design the living rooms look out on to the landscape around the house rather than in on the enclosed space. Wright designed every aspect of his creation, to the last detail of glass and the weave of the rugs that echo his spatial patterning (see the House for Susan Lawrence Dana page 42). The living room is a beautiful and restful space, under the hipped roof and using that as a ceiling, which gives the room a sense of shelter and also of lightness as though the visitor is in a tent. Extending out from the fireplace on both sides, Wright specified a forest mural, and that, with the art glass in the casement windows, conveys an atmosphere of forest light, shade and dappling.

HOUSE FOR STEPHEN M. B. HUNT, LA GRANGE, ILLINOIS 1907

Courtesy of Alan Weintraub/Arcaid

THIS house, designed on a square floorplan, is the realisation of a project that Wright presented first in July 1907 in the *Ladies Home Journal* as 'A Fireproof House for $5,000', as he had presented 'A Home in a Prairie Town' and 'A Small House with "lots of room in it"' in 1901. The 'fireproof house' of the article was designed to be built out of concrete, although this proved to be more expensive than the hopeful sum described by Wright. The cubic exterior of the house does not suggest the sense of space within, which the architect created by taking three-quarters of the floor space for living, in two dynamically linked areas that rotate round the central fireplace.

The entry to the house is narrow, and the visitor must turn at once to ascend stairs before entering the living room, which takes up half of the ground-floor area and is focused on the fireplace. The hearth is back at the centre of the house as it had been in the first version of Wright's own house in Oak Park (see page 14). The dining room flows from the living room on the other side of the fireplace, separated from it only by spatially suggestive beams on the ceiling. Here the dining room is larger than the quarter allowed by the article designs, so the kitchen pushes out on the limits of the cube. Wright gave the plans to the *Ladies Home Journal*, so that readers could write in for copies. Thus there were 'fireproof houses' built that had nothing to do with the architect, realising his hope for spreading his ideas as widely as possible.

HOUSE FOR F. F. TOMEK, RIVERSIDE, ILLINOIS *1907*

Courtesy of Alan Weintraub / Arcaid

THE Tomek house (planned in 1904) was, according to Wright, the precursor of the Robie house and the plans of the two houses have much in common. Here the red brick with the horizontal mortar lighter and deeply raked is on the inside rather than the outside, but the interior space is not as fully integrated as in its successor. The living and dining rooms are divided by a staircase, and there is no fireplace in the master bedroom, a later luxury the Robies benefited from.

As the visitor approaches the Tomek house, the Prairie features are clear, from the cantilevers to which Wright had to add non-load-bearing columns, as they needed visual if not structural reinforcement, to the raised windows that make it impossible to see what is happening inside from outside. Behind the right-hand wall is a billiard room, which is lit from the back of the house rather than from the windowless front.

HOUSE FOR E. E. BOYNTON, ROCHESTER, NEW YORK *1908*

Courtesy of William Allin Storrer (S, 147)

EDWARD Boynton, a widower with one daughter, knew of Wright's work through his partner Warren McArthur, whose sons worked with Wright on the Arizona Biltmore Hotel. Boynton approved of Wright's preference for designing the whole house down to its last fittings, and the original plumbing survived in the house at least until the early 1990s. The house originally had a veranda under a cantilevered extension but this was enclosed quite early on, using glass from the same supplier as was used for the rest of the house.

The dining room of this house is lit by an interesting combination of electric lights behind glass panels on the ceiling, in Robie-like holders on the walls, and daylight from the clerestorey windows. The original shower is memorable: a sunflower-like shower head is supported on metal piping that surrounds the generous foot plate and the whole contraption is ringed by tubular metal, giving a sense of enclosure – surely a great place to take a shower.

BLYTHE-MARKLEY CITY NATIONAL BANK AND HOTEL, MASON CITY, IOWA *1909*

Courtesy of the Frank Lloyd Wright Foundation

MARKLEY of Blythe-Markley was the father of one of the pupils at the Hillside Home School (see page 46) run by Wright's aunts. Wright provided a visually harmonious but spatially distinct solution to the challenge of creating a hotel and a bank on the same site. The Blythe-Markley building is composed of two distinct parts, which share features such as material, cantilevered roofs, horizontal dynamics and geometric patterning, but which are otherwise distinct according to their purposes.

The bank part of the lot is windowless at the ground-floor level, where the main banking hall and vaults are located, apart from basement lights, but it rises to a light and open-looking second floor that houses individual offices around a central hallway. The whole gives an impression of solidity and security that is well suited to its purpose. The hotel is set up in the opposite way, closed above and open below so that it is welcoming to its guests while offering them privacy once they are in their rooms. The floorplan is U-shaped, with the dining room in the central space of the U being lit from above by a skylit atrium that reaches up three floors to the roof level.

HOUSE FOR MRS THOMAS GALE, OAK PARK, ILLINOIS *1909*

Courtesy of William Allin Storrer (S.098)

THIS house, originally commissioned in 1904 but delayed by the death from cancer of Thomas Gale, is interesting as much for what it looks forward to as for what it is. By 1909 Wright had explored the Prairie idiom pretty thoroughly: indeed, towards the end of this year he was to leave Chicago, his wife, his architectural practice and his children, to go to Europe to seek inspiration and to publish some of his ideas more widely. However, much later on Wright himself saw this house as a precursor to one of his most famous works of all, Fallingwater (see page 134), and although Oak Park lacks the drama of the Bear Run site it is easy to see what he meant. Both structures are flat-roofed, without the hipped shelter that belongs to many of the Prairie houses, and both have dramatic cantilevered extensions that give them a kind of sculptural presence as well as an architectural one. However, in the end, this can only be judged to be a fine house, whereas Fallingwater is one of the great houses of the twentieth century, for reasons that will become apparent.

HOUSE FOR MEYER MAY, GRAND RAPIDS, MICHIGAN *1909*

Courtesy of the Frank Lloyd Wright Foundation

THIS beautiful Prairie house in Grand Rapids, Michigan displays a number of characteristically Wrightian features that are familiar to us already. For example, the windows are tucked under the eaves, and raised from ground level: here the ground-floor windows are so high that they light the stairwell and first-floor gallery and prohibit any intrusion by casual passers by.

The house is constructed out of pale brick, with a red roof, copper details and art-glass windows (see House for Arthur Heurtley page 44). Frank Lloyd Wright made use of an unusual device in the fireplace: he put gold art glass in between the courses of brick that made up the mantel so that the firelight flickered into the living room even when the flames were behind its brickwork. The decorative scheme is harmonious – the Wright-designed dining table is lit at each corner by art-glass lamps, and the pattern of the lamps is reiterated in the carpet and again in the sideboard.

HOUSE FOR GEORGE STEWART, MONTECITO, CALIFORNIA *1909*

Courtesy of Alan Weintraub/Arcaid

CONSTRUCTED from redwood board-and-batten, this is the only Prairie house in California, though it is not Wright's only design in the sunshine state (see House for John Storer page 116). The floorplan is a cruciform on a rigid 4-foot square grid, with two storeys, and the living room is a magnificent space that runs the full height of the house, with a balcony from the upstairs that overlooks the lower floor of the room. The shallow hipped roof and cantilevered extensions look different when surrounded by California's more verdant vegetation, but the use of local wood ensures that the house blends convincingly into its surroundings. The architect made easy and convincing use of multiple levels throughout the house to help define the different spaces, and in addition there are more physical barriers between the rooms than usual. It is striking that nearly a century later these Prairie houses are still eagerly sought by people as homes, a testament to their attractiveness as habitations.

TALIESIN I, SPRING GREEN, WISCONSIN AND TALIESIN II *1911 and 1914*

Courtesy of the Frank Lloyd Wright Foundation

IN 1909 Wright left his home, his family and his practice in Oak Park to go to Europe, to work on a portfolio of drawings for the German publisher Wasmuth and to be with Mamah Borthwick Cheney, the wife of a client, with whom he had become involved. His suburban lifestyle and successful architectural practice had come to seem constraining, and in Europe he not only studied architecture and read widely but also decided that his life must change despite his family feelings of affection compounded by guilt. On his return he began a building project that was still in progress on his death: the great masterpiece Taliesin in Wisconsin (see Taliesin III building, page 120).

Taliesin means 'shining brow' in Welsh, appropriate to the architect's plan for the building to emerge from the hill: 'It should be of the hill. Belonging to it.' In both the 1911 and the 1914 buildings he made use of local stone, gathered from the nearby river beds, and set in the walls as they had lain on the ground – uneven, patterned by erosion, solid and unmistakably organic. The sense of space is less obviously geometric but still harmonious. As usual Wright designed the furniture and glass for his new home, to which he added models of his own buildings and, of course, his collection of Japanese art.

As it exists today the building has little of the original 1911 structure; it was burned down in 1914 when an insane servant barricaded all the exits but one, set fire to the building and waited outside the only door with a hatchet. He not only destroyed Wright's home but also killed Mamah and her children. Wright began to rebuild immediately.

HOUSE FOR HARRY S. ADAMS, OAK PARK, ILLINOIS *1913*

Courtesy of the Frank Lloyd Wright Foundation

THIS was the last house that Wright built in Oak Park, and it is Prairie style to its final ornament. The art glass in the front door is particularly fine, and among Wright's custom-built furniture and fittings the copper ceiling-lights are especially beautiful. Light is as usual provided by a band of windows towards the top of each storey, all of which are casement-opening.

Wright much preferred casement windows to sash windows because the movement of opening them on their vertical hinges is an action that comes naturally to the human arm. With sash windows, on the other hand, there is an element of struggling against gravity; in addition, sashes do not open so far or afford such easily graded ventilation as do casements. Although the living areas in this house are open to each other, there is less a sense of fundamental unity of space here, with the entrance hall breaking them apart – as though the architect is no longer satisfied by the Prairie idiom and is looking towards his next challenge.

MIDWAY GARDENS, CHICAGO, ILLINOIS (DEMOLISHED) *1913*

Courtesy of the Frank Lloyd Wright Foundation

THIS glorious festival of buildings, and gardens for the summer and winter became financially untenable because of the economic challenges of the First World War and then Prohibition in 1920. In it Wright created a playground for the eye and a pleasure for the spirit that was designed to offer facilities for all kinds of music, for eating indoors and out and for dancing. The Imperial Hotel was imbued with much of this spirit in a different, more sober context (see page 106).

The site is 300 feet long and 300 feet deep, and in this square Wright planned a winter garden, housed in the main block, and a summer garden, which took up the majority of the ground space of the site and was a series of stepped courtyards that culminated in the bandstand at the back. The whole scheme was covered with decoration: brick, tile, stucco, coloured and patterned concrete blocks, stone and coloured glass, including sculpture as original as any in America and most in Europe at that time. It was lit with a profusion of geometrically placed electric lights that both advertised the attraction and illuminated it. The opening was an overwhelming success. Wright wrote: 'In a scene unforgettable to all who attended, the architectural scheme and colour, form, light and sound had come alive. And this scene came upon the beholders as a magic spell.'

HOUSE FOR SHERMAN BOOTH, GLENCOE, ILLINOIS *1915*

Courtesy of William Allin Storrer (S.187)

SHERMAN M. Booth was an attorney with big ideas who commissioned Wright to create a whole development close to a ravine just west of Glencoe that was to be named Ravine Bluffs. In the end six houses and three poured-concrete sculptures were created by the architect. Of the houses, five were to be rental properties, and four of these were variants of the 'fireproof house for $5,000' (see House for Stephen M. B. Hunt page 78). The building of the latter was not supervised by the architect.

The original, ostentatious, design for Booth's own house was abandoned in favour of extensive remodelling of an existing building. Its outward appearance has a kind of hybrid Prairie/$5,000 look, with a two-storey central block that shares the white-and-bordered massing of the Hunt house, although not its actual shape, but is surrounded by ground-hugging wings with overhanging eaves that feel more Prairie than anything else. Inside, the living spaces are generous, with copious built-in features by the architect: canopied beds, cupboards, drawers and bookcases, giving Wright's preferred integrated style of living.

HOUSE FOR E. D. BRIGHAM, GLENCOE, ILLINOIS *1915*

Courtesy of the Frank Lloyd Wright Foundation

THIS is the only version of the 'fireproof house' that Wright actually constructed in concrete. The House for E. D. Brigham was originally designed in 1908 while the architect was still residing in Oak Park, and when it was finally built Wright did not actually supervise its construction himself, although the builders working on the project did follow his specifications pretty closely.

The basic square floorplan of the house is expanded by two wings, and the central unit itself is not divided formally by walls; the reception area, living and dining spaces flow from one another with the space defined by piers. The fireplace sits centrally, opening on to the living area, which is expanded by a long enclosed porch to the south. Wright also made use of slit windows around the window bays on the ground floor, which give the bay piers the appearance of an individual mass set into the surrounding building, and which also give the room yet more light.

WAREHOUSE FOR A. D. GERMAN, RICHLAND CENTER, WISCONSIN *1915*

Courtesy of the Frank Lloyd Wright Foundation

AFTER the death of Mamah Borthwick Cheney in the fire at Taliesin in 1914, Frank Lloyd Wright became involved with a strong-willed and difficult woman called Miriam Noel, a self-consciously 'artistic' person who delighted in her liaison, and later tempestuous marriage, with the architect. Financial difficulties followed, and he designed this warehouse in his birthplace close to Taliesin in payment of a debt. It was intended to serve both as a storage space for Mr German's coal, grain, hay and cement stocks and also as place where he could sell these commodities, and it included premises for a restaurant, art gallery and retail shops. It was built of reinforced concrete which was faced with brick, with an elegant top storey decorated with geometric motifs reminiscent of South American prehistoric cultures. Wright found great inspiration in these over the next phase of his creative life (see Hollyhock House page 112).

HOUSE FOR FREDERICK C. BOGK, MILWAUKEE, WISCONSIN *1916*

Courtesy of the Frank Lloyd Wright Foundation

FREDERICK Bogk was the son of a butcher. He worked in land sales and insurance before making his name in politics, and through his professional life knew Arthur L. Richards (see page 108), who may have introduced him to Wright. However, it is also possible that the architect received the commission through the good offices of Mrs Bogk, who knew the Coonleys and had visited – and must have envied – their house in Riverside.

Although the floorplan of the house is not quite square, the distribution of space and the positioning of the fireplace at the house's core is reminiscent of Wright's earlier houses on a square base. However, the façade looks quite new and reveals a different aesthetic, one that has much in common with the Imperial Hotel on which Wright was working at the same time (see page 106), including brick-mullioned windows with a cast-concrete form sitting above them. The abstract shapes and mass of ornament, together with the overhanging eaves, give the house a pagoda-like air. Wright's enthusiasm for walnut dictated its use downstairs, although he used gum for the trim and furnishings on the upper floor.

IMPERIAL HOTEL AND IMPERIAL HOTEL ANNEX, TOKYO, JAPAN *1915, 1916*

Courtesy of the Frank Lloyd Wright Foundation

WRIGHT'S interest in Japanese art and design, evinced not only in his large collection of screens and sculptures but also in his writings (such as *The Japanese Print: An Interpretation*, 1912), took him to that country on a number of occasions. He described Japanese art as 'nearer to the earth and a more indigenous product of native conditions . . . therefore more nearly modern as I saw it, than any European civilisation'. In 1916, faced with debt and turmoil in the United States and with the challenge of a great commission, it was time for him and Miriam to set out again; for the next few years Wright divided his time between Japan, Wisconsin and California.

The Imperial Hotel is reminiscent of Midway Gardens (see page 96) in its grandeur of conception, its symmetrical central volume and the wings that grow from it to frame the central garden space. Unlike most of his buildings, however, the entrance is not hidden but is right in the middle of the structure, open to the street but surrounded both by the wings and by the light and reflection of the pool he positioned in the front courtyard. The soft Japanese Oya stone (lava) enabled an exceptional level of decorative carving to be included in the design and the three-storey entrance lobby (happily reconstructed in Meiji village after the demolition of the hotel itself) is a masterpiece of space, decoration and detail. Wright believed that the cantilevered base of the hotel's structure, complete with flexible joins resting on piles driven into the mud beneath (there was nothing solid to build the foundations on), enabled the hotel to survive the great earthquake of September 1923. It is quite probable that the hotel's location away from the epicentre also aided its survival.

DUPLEX APARTMENTS FOR RICHARDS COMPANY, MILWAUKEE, WISCONSIN *1916*

Courtesy of William Allin Storrer (S.201)

AS well as creating buildings for clients with a significant amount of money, Wright spent a great deal of time contemplating and drawing beautiful and affordable housing for the average American. The largest project of this nature was the 'American System Ready-Cut' of 1911–17, which consisted of nearly a thousand drawings and many built houses. The idea behind the project was that all these different buildings would be made from factory-created wooden walls, floor joists, roofs, windows, doors and trim, finished on site with stucco and plaster. He also designed all the furniture and finishes for mass production.

By a fortunate coincidence, Arthur L. Richards was a property developer who claimed that he could make large savings by building many houses at the same time, and Wright worked with him on this and other prefabricated projects such as the 'small house', the 'bungalow' and the 'two-storey house'. These duplex apartments are reminiscent of the new architecture in Europe at that time, built by designers such as Piet Mondrian: the blockiness and flat shapes in white with trim could have been made by Bauhaus designers. Inside, however, the Wright spatial freedom is very much in evidence, and it is interesting to see how he makes communal interaction vertical rather than horizontal through shared laundry spaces on the roof and entranceways for the whole block.

HOUSES FOR ARTHUR L. RICHARDS, MILWAUKEE, WISCONSIN *1916*

Courtesy of the Frank Lloyd Wright Foundation

LIKE the duplex apartments for Arthur Richards' construction company these two small houses belonged to the 'American System Ready-Cut' scheme.

The 'ready-cut' scheme was announced in the *Chicago Sunday Tribune* on 4 March 1917. The advertisement offered small houses from $2,750 to $3,500 and large ones from $5,000 to $100,000. Many suburban housing dealers were licensed to distribute them. The successful spread of these houses was, however, stopped by the outbreak of the First World War, which the United States entered only one month later. Of the whole project, five bungalows, eight duplex apartments and four two-storey houses were eventually built. With flat roofs, even the smallest ones had an early form of air-conditioning installed and all of them show his preoccupation with generous internal space and ease of movement.

HOLLYHOCK HOUSE FOR ALINE BARNSDALL, LOS ANGELES, CALIFORNIA *1917*

Courtesy of Natalie Tepper/Arcaid

ALINE Barnsdall was the granddaughter of William Barnsdall, an oil magnate from whom she inherited a considerable fortune. She wished to create a complex of buildings, including a house for herself, to accommodate a community of theatre people. Wright took her favourite flower as the key decorative motif, and he used the inspiring mass of the Mayan temple at Yucatán as an indigenous architecture to inspire the shaping of Hollyhock House. He described the complex as ideal for living 'like a princess in aristocratic seclusion'. The living room, music room and library make up a cruciform, and two wings run from it, one wide, with the bedrooms and a gallery, the other narrower with the dining room, kitchen and servants' accommodation. Between there is a garden court, and at the end of the complex he located a round pool, connected – in a new stroke of inspiration – to the fireplace in the living room and a square pool beyond it. The fireplace is extraordinary: lit from above by a skylight, the hearthstone is set into the pool so that the four ancient elements of fire, earth, air and water are united at the off-centred core of the house. The furniture that Wright designed echoes the ever-present hollyhock motif and looks, unusually, forbiddingly uncomfortable. This was not, however, a house designed solely for domestic comfort as it was semi-public: Ms Barnsdall held Bolshevik soirées.

Hollyhock House is also unusual in Wright's work because he set it on a hilltop to stand out from the landscape rather than to embrace it, although typically he insisted on the replanting of dead olive trees from the gridded orchard.

JIYU GAKUEN SCHOOL, TOKYO, JAPAN *1921*

Courtesy of William Allin Storrer (S.213)

JIYU Gakuen, or Free Spirit, school was one of the five designs that Wright made in Japan that were actually built (he planned five others that did not make it past the drawing board). Its floorplan is almost an exact reverse of the Hillside Home School buildings (see page 46), with the two masses connected by a passageway of classrooms: here there is a central mass of two storeys with 'Japanese' eaves reminiscent of the Susan Lawrence Dana house (see page 42) and two wings growing out from it to house the four classrooms. The main block housed the living/classroom, an assembly area on the ground floor and a dining room above the assembly room with a balcony over the large living space. Wright echoed the shape of the eaves in art glass in the mullioned windows, giving the large space a sense of geometric harmony and interest that must have made it an enjoyable room to be in when lessons were dull.

HOUSE FOR JOHN STORER *1923*

Courtesy of Alan Weintraub / Arcaid

JOHN Storer's was the second of four houses that Wright built out of textile block in California in 1923 (see page 118). In this house the ground floor holds the dining room and bedrooms and, unusually, the two-storey living room is above. One of the glories of this house are its terraces: one for the living room, built over the bedrooms, and others downstairs, including one with a trademark Wright pool bringing water close to the house.

For the first time the architect could exploit his grid system vertically as well as horizontally: in Wright's own words, 'Standardization was the soul of the machine, and here I was the weaver ... crocheting with it a free masonry fabric ... great in architectural beauty.'

Textile block was a good material to use in this climate, as it repelled heat in the summer and retained it in the winter – in other words, it acted as a good insulator. But textile block did not really look as though it belonged to the landscape in the way that Prairie brick or board-and-batten did, and with few windows and hidden doorways as well, these houses can be seen as somewhat isolationist, almost fortified constructions. Wright's second marriage (to Mamah Borthwick Cheney) was on its knees at the time this house was created and the architectural coolness of this phase of design was perhaps related to the loneliness of his personal life at this time. Wright's eldest son, Lloyd, supervised the construction of this and the other three textile-block houses in the state.

Textile-Block houses,
Los Angeles, California *1923*

Courtesy of Alan Weintraub / Arcaid

THE four textile-block houses (see House for John Storer page 116), and those for Charles Ennis, Alice Millard's La Miniatura, and the Freemans') that Wright built in California in 1923 have many similarities as well as some differences.

Obviously all four houses share the construction material, although each of them has a different pattern on the outer (display) faces of the blocks, and they all sit in dramatic sites over which they preside. The location of all of these houses means they enjoy magnificent views over Hollywood or the Santa Monica mountains. In fact they appear to be as much sculpture as house.

La Miniatura was the first of the four to be built – Alice Millard was a client who already had a Wright-designed Prairie house. The Ennis house is the largest of the four, and like the Hollyhock house (see page 112) it is reminiscent of a Mayan temple. The Ennis house suffered some structural problems because Wright used decomposed granite to colour the blocks, and this caused the concrete to decay. The Freeman house and Storer house (pictured opposite) were smaller, but they were set more closely into the landscape, growing down the hills they were built on to reveal lower levels than suggested by the entrance. Lloyd, the architect's eldest son, supervised the construction of all three houses. Wright found the mechanisation of his building through this material deeply satisfying: he described it as 'tough, light, but not "thin", imperishable, plastic; no necessary lie about it anywhere and yet machine-made, mechanically perfect.'

TALIESIN III, SPRING GREEN, WISCONSIN *1925*

Courtesy of the Frank Lloyd Wright Foundation

WRIGHT'S home in Wisconsin suffered three times from fire: the first caused by an electrical fault, the second arson, the third probably a lightning strike. Each time Wright rebuilt, expanded, developed his vision and tied his house more closely to its hill and its landscape. He even dammed the river to form a lake, so water became more of a feature in its outlook as well as being pumped to the house and in the courtyard. The 1925 fire, like that of 1914, struck the living quarters, but after this he not only recovered the lost parts of the house but also added considerably to the westward part. This highlights a difficulty for those who live and work in, and seek to preserve, his domestic creations – all the time they were in flux, whereas historical preservation likes to see one fixed moment of being for the re-creation to restore. Wright's vision of living, developing buildings does not sit easily with this.

The 1925 sections were, like the rest of the complex, built of limestone, plaster and wood. The house sits around its courtyard, where Wright kept ancient trees as part of the harmony of the site. The visitor arrives around the hill, through the lakes, into the courtyard that is surmounted by the hilltop, so that the landscape truly embraces the house with it organic and harmonious grounding in the materials of its neighbourhood.

ARIZONA BILTMORE HOTEL
AND COTTAGES, PHOENIX, ARIZONA 1927

Courtesy of the Frank Lloyd Wright Foundation

THIS was the next commission for which Wright used concrete blocks (see the textile-block houses, page 118) although strictly speaking the project was not truly his own; he was approached by the MacArthur brothers, sons of an Oak Park client, who needed some assistance with the project for a resort hotel that they were working on in the Arizona desert. They looked to the architect for input in some aspects of the design, particularly in the design of the major interior spaces. The MacArthur brothers paid Wright $10,000 simply for the privilege of using the textile-block system of construction, as they were under the impression that it was patented technology.

The work of Frank Lloyd Wright can, however, be easily detected in the design of the lobby, with its geometric massing and familiar balcony, as well as in the cottages, sitting on their square grids. However, Albert MacArthur tinkered somewhat with the design in an attempt to save money and his interventions upset the clarity of the complex's geometry. Nonetheless, the building still has a number of notable features. Among these are the the largest gold-leafed ceiling in the world (in the lobby) and a roof which is constructed out of an almost unbelievable 32,500 pounds of copper. And, of course, the blocks, and the geometry, are still reminiscent of the master.

GREYCLIFF HOUSE FOR ISABEL, MRS DARWIN D. MARTIN, DERBY, NEW YORK *1927*

Courtesy of Alan Weintraub / Arcaid

IT was not enough for the Martins to have one of the largest, and finest, Prairie houses (see page 54); Mrs Martin decided that she would also like a Wright-designed summer house. The Martins were good friends to Wright, and not only as patrons. When the Bank of Wisconsin foreclosed on his $43,000 debt in 1928 they became stockholders of Wright, Inc., the company that Wright formed to hold Taliesin and his other assets, so that he could get on with thinking up new architectural projects in the company of his new wife, Olgivanna.

All this was still to come, however, when the architect designed this homely and comfortable residence just above Lake Erie. Its living room, furnished by 'Bel' in un-Wrightian wicker, is dominated by a fireplace formed from large stones, reminiscent of those of the Lake Delavan cottages (see page 34). It also has a screened sleeping porch, to allow some relief from the baking summers. The family much enjoyed spending long periods here over the summer.

HOUSE FOR RICHARD LLOYD JONES, TULSA, OKLAHOMA *1929*

Courtesy of the Frank Lloyd Wright Foundation

DURING the bad times of the 1920s Wright was glad of this commission from his cousin Richard, editor of the *Tulsa Tribune*, who had also supported him financially when he did not have enough work.

The house is built on a 5-foot square grid, around a courtyard (like Taliesin), with a swimming pool and fishpond. It is made of glass and textile block and more so than with most of Wright's work, it is comparable with what the modernists were doing in Europe at the time. The architect never acknowledged the influence of designers such as Mies van de Rohe, Walter Gropius, Gerrit Rietveld or Piet Mondrian, although they knew of his work from the *Wasmuth Portfolios* and the Dutch architect Widjeveld's *The Life-Work of the American Architect Frank Lloyd Wright*, published in 1925. It is hard to ignore the connections between this building, as well as the Californian textile-block houses, and those of the modernists, built in what is known as the International style. The modular definition of rooms and the essential blockiness of the design, without the ground-hugging sense of belonging that had extended from the Prairie houses to Taliesin, make these houses seem different from his earlier and later works. However, this marked a time of transition for Wright whose style was evolving into his second great creative contribution of this kind, the Usonian house.

TALIESIN FELLOWSHIP COMPLEX, SPRING GREEN, WISCONSIN *1932*

Courtesy of the Frank Lloyd Wright Foundation

FRANK Lloyd Wright believed that the architect should be at the heart of the planning of housing, whether urban, suburban or rural. As time went by he came to believe that the city was dead and that the future lay in a decentralised America, best expressed in the model of Broadacre City (see page 132). The model was built by his own planned community, the group of trainees that he gathered around him at his Spring Green home in 1932 that he called the Taliesin Fellowship.

He housed his new fellowship in the redesigned buildings of Hillside Home School, which he had inherited on the death of his aunts. The Fellowship was not to be a conventional school; rather, novices would learn from experienced people the skills of moulding and casting, pottery, weaving, drama, and, of course, the principles of organic architecture would be taught by the master himself. They would also spend time working in the fields and gardens of Taliesin to promote self-sufficiency in food, and on the various building projects that were ongoing in the complex. The fee for this apprenticeship was announced as $650 per year.

The drafting studio is an extraordinary horizontal space whose beams run vertically and diagonally at two different angles (based on the equilateral triangle and a narrower, sharper dynamic), as well as horizontally. This creates an impression that the room is a forest, an impression reinforced by the sourcing of the light from a clerestory up in the ceiling. At the same time the space is like a cloister, with a raised flagstone floor running around the edge – a remarkable interplay that makes it a superb room for its purpose.

HILLSIDE PLAYHOUSE, SPRING GREEN, WISCONSIN 1933

Courtesy of the Frank Lloyd Wright Foundation

ALONG with the drafting room, Wright's apprentices built a playhouse out of the old Hillside Home School buildings. This was opened to the public on Sunday afternoons from November 1933; people could come to watch a movie for 50 cents, after which they could have a cup of tea and a doughnut with Mrs Wright and, if they were lucky, talk to the architect himself.

The playhouse was built inside the existing cruciform volume of the old school gymnasium, with three banks of seats at the lower level and balconies echoing that shape above. The visitor enters the building from the rear of the stage, like the behind-the-podium entrance in Unity Temple (see page 56), and then walks through a constrained space before reaching the open theatre space itself. The balcony is suspended, a technique that Wright used again in Florida Southern College's chapel a few years later.

Despite critical comment that Wright was merely getting help from foolish paying assistants to undertake maintenance of his property in the face of his own poverty, the Fellowship was oversubscribed. Despite raising the annual fee to $1,100 and lowering the numbers of apprentices to 30, Wright had 27 people on his waiting list by the end of 1932. Some people learned a great deal, some found the hierarchy forbidding and left disillusioned, but it is impressive that, whatever the faults of the Fellowship, the practice of architecture continues at Taliesin to this day.

MODEL FOR
BROADACRE CITY *1934*

Courtesy of the Frank Lloyd Wright Foundation

WRIGHT was preoccupied throughout his life with the question of urban planning, and before the 1930s had engaged with schemes for groups of houses as well as individual dwellings. In 1934 he was invited to present a city of the future for an exhibition in New York. His friend Edgar Kaufmann gave him the money to build, with the Taliesin apprentices, not only a model of four square miles of a new city but also the drawings and models of individual buildings that would be its constituent parts.

Broadacre City is actually misnamed, because it was not a city at all. Wright believed that the days of the old-fashioned urban conglomerate were over and that the future held a new way of living, decentralised, without state or city. This new society would be based on the county, autonomous apart from the functions of defence, international trade regulation and diplomacy, for which it would be linked directly to national government. All other functions would be governed at local level, kept to a scale that meant that all citizens could participate: schools, roads, commerce, multi-faith centres of worship, justice, policing and recreation. Of course, the architect was to be the highest official. The fundamental unit of this city was the 1-acre tract of land with a Usonian house on it, and with this would go universal car ownership. As an ideal, Broadacre could never be realised, but it contributed to the debate on urban development. It is widely recognised that cities are better without cars in the communal areas, as Broadacre suggested; its clusters of commercial enterprise foreshadowed malls; and its pollution-free factories looked forward to industrial zones around major cities.

FALLINGWATER HOUSE FOR EDGAR J. KAUFMANN, BEAR RUN, PENNSYLVANIA 1935

Courtesy of the Frank Lloyd Wright Foundation

THIS house, one of the most famous of domestic dwellings, is one of Wright's greatest achievements and a beautiful, breathtaking and inspiring creation. Edgar J. Kaufmann was a very rich man, whose son was an apprentice at Taliesin. It was therefore natural for him to ask Wright to create a house on some land the family owned in the Pennsylvania forests. Wright apparently asked where on the estate Kaufmann liked to sit, and when he was shown the rock above the Bear Run's shooting waterfall he declared that that very stone should be the hearthstone of the house.

Wright integrated much of his earlier design invention in this house, himself citing the Gale house for the projecting balconies from slab-like walls as a precedent, but it is of itself utterly new and different. The core of the house, the living spaces, are quite simple and not enormous: a good-sized living room and compact kitchen on the main floor and three neat bedrooms above. It is the cantilevered terraces, shooting out with barely contained energy at a series of right angles, that make the house look like sculpture as well as architecture and that give it its extraordinary character. Although today the building has a few structural problems, these double cantilevered extensions are sound, a tribute to the engineering skills of Wright and his associates, Mendel Glickman and William Wesley Peters.

HOUSE FOR HERBERT JACOBS, MADISON, WISCONSIN *1936*

Courtesy of William Allin Storrer (S.234)

THIS, the first completely Usonian house, was built on a 2-foot by 4-foot rectangular grid, on an L-shaped floorplan with the quiet area on the long part of the 'L' and the living area on its base. The workspace and bathroom occupy the corner, and there is a dining area close by that links the workspace to the living room. This plan puts the new American housewife at the heart of the house where she can join in activities in the living space and also be aware of what is happening in the quiet area.

The base of the house is a thin concrete slab, which rests on a gravel bed that holds iron steam or hot-water pipes for 'gravity' heating under the floors and up the walls, so radiators are no longer needed. The grid mentioned above allowed the contractor to build easily (doors and windows had never been so easy to place) and with a minimum of material waste (for example, plywood came in 4-foot cuts). The walls were simple to make – a plywood core with waterproofing on each side, covered by one-foot boards battened on – and also energy efficient as they were good for insulation as well as being cheap and strong. Some have been reminded of the cottages that Wright built over thirty years before. The roof is a slab with a 12-inch cavity within it for further insulation and, as it hangs over the edge of the building, it does not need gutters. The architect thought of the automobile as weatherproof so he introduced the carport, a covered but not enclosed space on the outside of the 'L'.

HONEYCOMB HOUSE FOR PAUL R. AND JEAN HANNA, STANFORD, CALIFORNIA *1936*

Courtesy of Alan Weintraub / Arcaid

ALTHOUGH the Hanna house, known as the Honeycomb House because of the hexagonal grid on which it is designed, is larger and more expensive than most of Usonian houses, it belongs with them stylistically. Wright came to the view that the hexagon was more natural than the square, and that 'all things in nature exhibit this tendency to crystallise – to form and then conform . . . there is a fluid, elastic period of becoming . . . when possibilities are infinite.'

As the house was on a larger scale it offered the architect extra scope, and he designed the plan around a courtyard that contained an oak rather like the one at Taliesin. Because of the ease of construction of the walls it was easy for the house to be rearranged to suit the family's changing needs – when the children left home the living space was simply enlarged, as their rooms were no longer needed. It is also interesting to note that Wright gave the kitchen an extra, doubling roof above the main one so that it could be vented, allowing the circulation of fresh air. Lighting on the street side came from a clerestory just below the ceilings so that they seem to float, and from enormous windows opening on to the courtyard garden space.

S. C. JOHNSON AND SON INC. (JOHNSON WAX) ADMINISTRATION BUILDING, RACINE, WISCONSIN *1936*

Courtesy of William Allin Storrer (S.237)

THIS, like the Larkin Company Building (see page 52) is an extraordinary solution to a commercial building challenge. Wright was concerned throughout his career with making places of work environments that would be just as enjoyable to inhabit and move about in as any public space, such as galleries, museums and places of worship. By 1936, the company Johnson and Son Inc. had been profit-sharing with employees for nearly twenty years, and it had an excellent reputation for enlightened management. The building Wright created would complement the company's overall philosophy and would add to employee benefits; this Johnson company building is indeed an amazing place to work.

The great workroom, 120 feet by 200 feet by 25 feet high, is made unique by the columns that Wright designed to hold up the roof. These elegant creations, with a mere 9-inch-diameter base, open out to an 18-foot disk, capable of bearing five times the load that the Wisconsin State Building Commission demanded. Wright had a column cast and then staged a public test in which the column, laden with 60 tons of sandbags, sand and spoil, broke only when one of the non-load-bearing braces was knocked away. As so often in his public buildings there are no windows offering views, but light is provided by pyrex tubes of varying dimensions that make up the standard width of a brick plus mortar. He also designed all the furniture, with desks including built-in wastepaper baskets.

WINGSPREAD HOUSE FOR HERBERT F. JOHNSON, RACINE, WISCONSIN *1937*

Courtesy of William Allin Storrer (S.239)

HERBERT F. Johnson was a great patron for Wright, although their relationship didn't get off to the most auspicious start: when they first met to discuss the Johnson Building the only point of agreement they could find between them concerned their cars: they both drove Lincoln Zephyrs. After commissioning Wright to create the office building, Herbert F. Johnson approached the architect and asked him to build him a house. The Wingspread House that Wright created was described by him the architect as the last of the Prairie houses and also as 'a tall central brick chimney stack with five fireplaces on four sides'.

This stack was housed in the central three-storey octagon, inspired by the native American teepee. The floorplan is pinwheel, with four wings. The playroom is set at a 45-degree angle and the end of the swimming pool is cut off in the same way, so there is a sense of Wright's later geometry in the house as well as a sense of its Prairie roots.

OFFICE FOR
EDGAR J. KAUFMANN,
PITTSBURGH, PENNSYLVANIA *1937*

*Courtesy of the Victoria and Albert Museum,
London / Bridgeman Art Library*

AS well as his great house Fallingwater (see page 134), Edgar Kaufmann commissioned Wright to work on his department store in Pittsburgh. Wright continued to seek harmony and integration between architecture, décor and furniture, and as the Larkin Building and the Johnson Wax Building show, he carried this concern for aesthetic and functional unity into the workplace as much as the home. This office (now on display at the Victoria and Albert Museum in London) evokes and resolves many of these preoccupations in its unity of beauty, form and function in miniature.

The furniture is made of cedar wood, and on the wall behind the leaved table that serves as a desk there is a mural of abstract geometric patterns made from the same material, which echoes and reinforces its angular elegance and peaceful colouring. The carpet and upholstery were handwoven with an asymmetrical pattern of yellow and off-white that completes the effect.

TALIESIN WEST, SCOTTSDALE, ARIZONA *1937*

Courtesy of Alan Weintraub / Arcaid

WRIGHT'S fascination with the desert began in the 1920s through his work in California, and his first building in the state was the Arizona Biltmore hotel (see page 122). In 1929 he moved to the desert for the winter to avoid the rigours of Wisconsin's climate – he was, after all, sixty-two by now. After a bout of pneumonia in 1936, he decided to locate the Fellowship there during the winter months.

The complex of buildings designed and built by Wright for and with the Fellowship seems to grow organically from the rough soil around it. The principal material is 'desert rubblestone wall', lumps of rock joined with mortar, with redwood beams above to serve as frames for the linen canvas that proved to be the best material for shelter and which diffused light in desert winters. Each year the canvas was renewed as part of the annual move; it was set on the frames with hinges so that the breezes of the desert could be captured and enjoyed.

The complex continued to grow, with the original wooden building for Mr and Mrs Wright being converted into a permanent house, Sun Cottage, in 1948, and with a new cabaret theatre being added for lectures and social events in 1949. The Fellowship still travels south for the winter.

FLORIDA SOUTHERN COLLEGE, ADMINISTRATION BUILDINGS, LAKELAND, FLORIDA *1945, 1948*

Courtesy of the Frank Lloyd Wright Foundation

THERE are two major differences between Florida Southern College as specified by Wright and as it physically exists. His aerial perspective showed a citrus grove, planted on a grid, all around the buildings so that the esplanades that joined them would be pathways through lush leaves and the buildings would seem to float above a sea of green – similar to the scheme for David Wright's house (see page 200). All the college buildings made during his lifetime have exposed concrete brick bases, up to the level the fruit trees would have reached, and they are linked by esplanades (covered walkways that also serve as breezeways in the hot Florida summers). The trees were never planted. The administrative buildings are grouped around a pool, giving a courtyard effect that is completed by a double esplanade. The second major difference is that Wright's drawing linked the campus to the lake by positioning an amphitheatre and a swimming pool at the bottom of the slope – the pool being half in and half out of the larger body of water. It is a pity that his vision was not realised.

Florida Southern College, Pfeiffer Chapel, Lakeland, Florida *1938*

Courtesy of the Frank Lloyd Wright Foundation

FLORIDA Southern College is the largest group of buildings by Frank Lloyd Wright in existence. Dr Ludd M. Spivey was president of Florida Southern and he asked Wright to create a college of tomorrow. Wright obliged with an overall scheme and designs for twelve individual buildings; all of them are based on a 6-foot-square grid.

Since this is a Methodist liberal arts establishment, the Annie Merner Pfeiffer Chapel was the first building to be constructed. The geometry here is hexagonal, with the lower level making an even cruciform with points both on the end with the altar and on the one opposite, whereas upstairs the long axis runs across the building, with extra seating all around; the choir is positioned above the altar. The chapel has a dramatic bell tower over the main hall, which brings light pouring in through the clear glass. Like Unity Temple (see page 56), the space is lit from above and there are no external windows.

FLORIDA SOUTHERN COLLEGE, ROUX LIBRARY, LAKELAND, FLORIDA *1941*

Courtesy of the Frank Lloyd Wright Foundation

THE E. T. Roux Library must have seemed like a futuristic fantasy when Wright proposed it: the fabulous sweep of the study terraces, lit by a cunning arrangement of clerestory and beam, looks like a 1950s-style UFO rather than what we think of as a library. The circular study area grows from the pentagonal book storage area in such a way that the librarian is both on one point of the pentagon and right at the centre of the circle, with the trademark Wrightian fireplace behind, in the pentagon's centre. The book stacks stretch behind and below, lit by light wells. The library no longer houses books; it is not big enough for the College's collection, so it is now used by administrators. The architect returned to the ancient idea of a shape within a circle in a way reminiscent of this library when he designed the Annunciation Greek Orthodox Church in Wauwatosa (see page 224).

'SUNTOP' HOMES, ARDMORE, PENNSYLVANIA *1938*

Courtesy of the Frank Lloyd Wright Foundation

WRIGHT created a number of designs for grouped housing throughout his career. While he was working on the ideas for Broadacre City (see page 132), he came up with several four-house clusters, all of which are designed to sit on a single site, facing away from each other on a pinwheel plan. This gave each of the families privacy, views across their own yards and a sense of space.

The Suntop homes for Otto Mallery and the Todd Company are spread over three storeys, with the living room and carport sharing the ground floor and a mezzanine above (main bedroom, kitchen/dining area, bathroom, nursery) that reaches only halfway across the main room, so that it is two storeys high. Then, on the top floor, are the children's rooms and the sun terrace, closed off from its neighbours by board sidings. Wright planned four of these blocks but the locals complained so only one was built – he saw similar blocks completed in North Carolina (with the car outdoors and a one-storey living room), but the scheme's second proposed incarnation, in Massachusetts, was foiled by local architects.

AULDBRASS PLANTATION AND HOUSE FOR C. LEIGH STEVENS, YEMASSEE, SOUTH CAROLINA *1938 onwards*

Courtesy of William Allin Storrer (S.261)

LEIGH Stevens approached Wright because he wanted a working farm where he could test agricultural techniques that could then be exported overseas. The plans called for his own house, seven cottages, stabling for cows, mules and horses, chicken runs, a granary, kennels, quarters for a caretaker, a shop and a manager's office.

Wright set the walls of these buildings, made of native cypress, at 80 degrees rather than at the conventional 90, in order to echo the oak trees on the property, and he linked all the buildings together with esplanades attached to the walls, rather than freestanding as at Florida Southern College (see page 148). The Stevens house and the two cottages that made it off the drawing board are built on a hexagonal grid. The living-room windows have a rather lovely patterning, of rectangles set across at an angle to highlight the offset of the walls in a pleasing geometry.

HOUSE FOR ALMA GOETSCH AND KATHERINE WINKLER, OKEMOS, MICHIGAN *1939*

Courtesy of the Frank Lloyd Wright Foundation

EIGHT Michigan State University professors formed a co-op in the 1930s and bought a tract of land: two of them, Alma Goetsch and Katherine Winkler, approached Wright and asked him to design the site for them. He came up with a scheme arising directly from the Broadacre concept (see page 132), to be known as Usonia I: seven Usonian houses and a caretaker's cottage surrounding a farm, fish pond and orchard held in common. Financing collapsed, so the Goetsch–Winkler house was the only one built.

The house is a so-called 'in-line Usonian', literally a house built in a straight line on a 4-foot-square grid. The living room/studio takes up much of the house, with a gallery running along behind the two bedrooms, separated by a bathroom; both open out on to a veranda. At the other end of the living room is a brick wall that contains a fireplace and chimney, creating an alcove with bookshelves; behind this wall is the workspace.

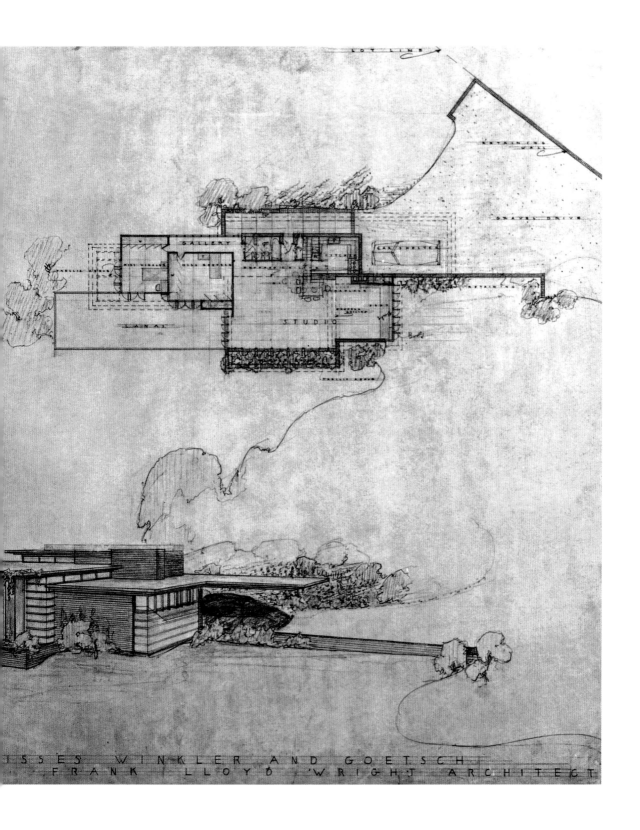

MISSES WINKLER AND GOETSCH
FRANK LLOYD WRIGHT ARCHITECT

GATEHOUSE FOR ARCH OBOLER, RETREAT FOR ELEANOR OBOLER & HOUSE FOR ARCH OBOLER
1940, 1941 & 1955

Courtesy of the Frank Lloyd Wright Foundation

ARCH Oboler commissioned Wright to build him a magnificent complex, to be called Eaglefeather, leaping from a Malibu precipice towards the Pacific on cantilevers of the kind used in Fallingwater. Unfortunately, the financial insecurity of Arch's movie business (he was big in 3-D films) meant that the funds were not there to build the dream, so he and his wife Eleanor lived in the gatehouse Wright built them instead, until Arch could afford a less grandiose scheme in 1955.

Like Taliesin West (see page 146), the stone parts of the Gatehouse were constructed of desert rubblestone wall, with wooden sidings that seem to rise naturally from the rocky scrub site. Eleanor Oboler's retreat, which was built close by in the Santa Monica mountains, looks out across the magnificent and desolate landscape that must have appealed to Wright, given his great affection for the desert of Arizona.

HOUSE FOR THEODORE BAIRD, AMHERST, MASSACHUSETTS *1940*

Courtesy of William Allin Storrer (S.277)

LIKE the Goetsch–Winkler house, this is an in-line Usonian house, remarkable for a number of special features. It was the only one of the Usonian designs for which the materials were actually prefabricated before being brought to the site. Usually the board-and-batten constructions were cut into pieces and assembled when the house was being built, but for this house a New Jersey contractor prepared the materials at his factory before delivery. The house is constructed of a mixture of cypress wood and brick, and its interior arrangement is rather unusual. The generously proportioned living room has a fireplace at one end, placed in a partition that divides the open part of the room, creating an area beyond it that is a kind of snug, the so-called sanctum. This in turn is heated by a second grate, which backs on to the first. At the other end of the house the master bedroom also has a fireplace: the house must have been extremely snug during all those chilly Massachusetts winters.

SNOWFLAKE HOUSE FOR CARLTON D. WALL, DETROIT, MICHIGAN 1941

Courtesy of the Frank Lloyd Wright Foundation

AS Wright explored the spatial opportunities of the hexagon and the triangle (see the Honeycomb House, page 112), he discovered the capacity of the 30-, 60- and 120-degree angles to make more interesting and different interiors, proportions and boundaries around the spaces that his clients lived in.

Here for the first time the architect used the 60/120-degree equilateral parallelogram (that is, a diamond or a square squashed on its side; if you cut the square in half through the large angles you get two equilateral triangles, with all corners having 60-degree angles – this is a very stable shape.) The house gets its name from its aerial view, where the wings radiate out from the living area, the central hexagon of the building. (The angles of a hexagon are all 120 degrees.) Wright divides this in a way somewhat reminiscent of his original square house: the living room takes up half the space, the dining room just over a quarter and the workspace and bathroom the other quarter. The dining room has two hexagonal goldfish ponds, under segmented hexagonal lights, which make explicit Wright's constant preoccupation with outdoor and indoor space meeting.

SOLAR HEMICYCLE HOUSE FOR HERBERT JACOBS, MIDDLETON, WISCONSIN *1944*

Courtesy of the Frank Lloyd Wright Foundation

IF Wright could make use of octagons, hexagons, squares, triangles and parallelograms in his buildings, then why not circles? This is the first of the solar hemicycle houses that Wright designed, so-called because they take advantage of the position and movement of the sun throughout the course of the day.

These solar houses could be either concave on their private face, like this one for Herbert Jacobs, or convex. The segments of the house are of 6 degrees of arc, and Wright positioned the living quarters up on a balcony over the living room so there is no gallery joining the living and quiet zones. The inside of the arc is composed of a glassed 'windowall' (a wall made up of windows) that looks out on to a terrace. A pool joins the inner and outer space here – the same feature can be seen in the Snowflake House for Carlton D. Wall (see page 164). The outer face of this house is set in to a berm so that the earth protects it from the extremes of the Wisconsin winter weather.

S. C. JOHNSON AND SON INC.
(JOHNSON WAX) RESEARCH TOWER, RACINE, WISCONSIN *1944*

Courtesy of ESTO

THIS remarkable tower is, with the Johnson Wax Administration Building (see page 140) next door, a national American landmark. Wright decided to use a particularly innovative feature for this building: for the first time he used cantilevers in a tower, so that the walls do not bear any load – just as they did not in the Romeo and Juliet windmill tower (see page 26).

Wright designed the research tower so that all the communal utilities – the lifts, stairs, water supply and drainage – are located together in a central core, and in another extraordinary and inventive turn of design he made the floors alternately round and square. This meant that the round floors did not reach the walls of the building and consequently workers were able to communicate with each other from one floor to the next. This design solution fostered close relationships between the research chemists working there and was very much in keeping with Wright's philosophy that places of work should be enjoyable spaces to inhabit and within which colleagues should be able to communicate freely and happily with each other. The research tower is supported by a 'tap root' core that reaches over 50 feet below ground level to a thick concrete slab, 60 feet in diameter, which tapers towards the edge so that the building is utterly stable.

HOUSE FOR LOWELL WALTER, CEDAR ROCK, QUASQUETON, IOWA, AND RIVER PAVILION *1945*

Courtesy of the Frank Lloyd Wright Foundation

THE Second World War interrupted Wright's sensational surge of creativity from the 1930s, and this design had to wait five years from drawing board to build because of the restrictions on the supply of building materials imposed by post-war austerity. Based on another design, this time for a glass house, that he propagated through the pages of the *Ladies Home Journal*, the house consists of a long quiet zone culminating in a workspace, with a large garden room adjoining it set at an angle of 120 degrees. The grid is based on a 63-inch square, the only use of this odd-seeming unit in Wright's work. The pierced cantilevered roof reaches one square over the surrounding area, and the architect specified the use of planters to link inner and outer spaces in this area, reminiscent of the plants he specified as far back as the Prairie houses (see House for Frederick C. Robie page 74). Further down towards the Wapsipinicon river is a pavilion/boathouse, built of the same brick and on a grid of the same-sized squares, but with screens rather than glass.

HOUSE FOR DOUGLAS GRANT, CEDAR RAPIDS, IOWA 1946

Courtesy of Alan Weintraub / Arcaid

FRANK Lloyd Wright was known for a number of personal eccentricities. One of these was his letter-writing style, which was highly idiosyncratic and tended on occasion towards the most extreme brevity. When the Grant family first wrote to the architect on the subject of whether it was possible for him to plan a house for them, his reply was short to say the least, but it was the answer they were looking for: 'Dear Grants, Of course its possible'.

The house he created for the Grants is made from stone that came from the quarry on their own property. This house is another in-line Usonian, like the House for Alma Goetsch and Katherine Winkler (see page 158) or the House for Theodore Baird (see page 162), and is constructed on a 4-foot-square grid with a two-storey living room and the entrance upstairs.

The visitor enters the house at the loggia and then can turn left and go down the back stairs, ending up in the utilities space that leads on to the workspace. Alternatively, the main staircase of the house runs down a dramatically narrow corridor, (opposite) which is lit only by a clerestory in the public façade, towards the open, well-lit space of the living room at the other end. This house shows a typically Wrightian manipulation of light and space – one which can be traced directly from the architect's early works and which was a feature of his building design throughout his career (see Unity Temple page 56).

House for Dr Alvin Miller, Charles City, Iowa *1946*

Courtesy of Alan Weintraub/Arcaid

THIS Usonian house, built of stone and cypress wood, is located close to the Cedar River, Iowa. Wright took great care to orientate the house so that it would take best advantage of the views its river location afforded.

Most of Frank Lloyd Wright's L-shaped Usonians, for example the House for Herbert Jacobs (see page 136), tended to look inwards on the 'L' over the garden that filled the right-angle. In this house for Dr Alvin Miller, however, Wright extended the long arm of the 'L' and located the main enclosed area in that second corner space, looking out towards the river. This has the effect of detaching the quiet zone further from the house. The extra wing also gave the living room an even greater sense of privacy. Characteristically, the building seems to emanate from the ground, as its wooden roof supports and stone chimney blending harmoniously with the surrounding landscape of Iowa, just as Wright had intended.

Unitarian Meeting House, Shorewood Hills, Wisconsin *1947*

Courtesy of William Allin Storrer (S.291)

WRIGHT was asked by the First Unitarian Society of Madison, Wisconsin, to design a new building for their worship in 1946. It took him eighteen months to come up with the fieldstone and glass triangle design. It was built for $165,000 plus a lot of effort on the part of the parishioners, who carried the stone from the quarry themselves to save on cost.

This is another Wright building where it is easy to see evidence of what has gone before at the same time as appreciating its great originality and its appropriateness for the purpose for which it was designed. The dynamic glass apse, sheltered by the folded copper roof, is reminiscent of the bell tower of the Annie Pfeiffer Chapel at Florida Southern College (see page 150). Here, however, the soaring roof forestalls the need for a separate bell space; its dramatic height and embracing low eaves provide for everything to be sheltered beneath it. Wright later compared the prow-like apse and sheltering eaves to the hands of a supplicant in prayer emerging from their habit.

HOUSE FOR MAYNARD BUEHLER, ORINDA, CALIFORNIA *1948*

Courtesy of Alan Weintraub/Arcaid

THE standard materials used for this house for Maynard Buehler in California are concrete block and wood. These materials belie the unexpected shape of the living room, which emerges from the standard in-line shape of the main part of the house as an octagon under a rectangular roof set at 45 degrees to the main space. This sets up the first of the 135-degree angles of the octagon, which is surrounded by casement windows. In addition, the roof over the octagon is itself sloping. This means that not only are the angles of the walls surprising but the room also expands and contracts vertically, thereby creating an unusual multi-dimensional energy that must have made the Buehler house an extremely interesting place in which to live. It is also typical of Wright's Usonian houses of this period, for example the House for Ward McCartney (see page 192). At the other end of the house is the workshop that Mr Buehler used to invent new accessories for guns.

HOUSE FOR SOL FRIEDMAN, USONIA II, PLEASANTVILLE, NEW YORK *1948*

Courtesy of the Frank Lloyd Wright Foundation

LIKE Galesburg Country Homes and Parkwyn Village (page 190) Usonia II was intended to be an incarnation of the idea of Broadacre City.

Inspired by a Taliesin apprentice, a group of friends joined together and incorporated themselves as the Rochdale Cooperative in 1944. The coop purchased land in Pleasantville and retained Wright to design all the buildings, although in fact he limited himself to three and a supervisory role, the rest being created by apprentices and followers. Although these homes do not have wooden walls they are still Usonian – the stone was local and cheap and so fulfilled the criterion of economy just as well as wood did in other circumstances.

Sol Friedman's house is the most dashing, composed of two interlocking cylinders of 18-degree segments, in multiples of 6 feet, a larger one-storey and a smaller two-storey that fits on to it. The hearth is in the middle of the complex, and the living space unsurprisingly takes up about half of the larger cylinder. This house shares geometry with the Jacobs hemicycle house (see page 166) – it is the hemicycle completed, and a spatial tour de force.

HOUSE FOR JACK LAMBERSON, OSKALOOSA, IOWA *1948*

Courtesy of Alan Weintraub/Arcaid

LIKE the Hanna Honeycomb house for Paul R. and Jean Hanna (see page 138), Wright's design approach for this dramatic and beautiful building was to avoid the right angle wherever possible: both the carport and the living room have dramatic triangular cantilevers that seem to thrust upwards from the rolling hilltop site, while still being anchored firmly to their setting.

The central masonry core of the House for Jack Lamberson is built of brick. It is this core that seems to prevent the house from taking flight: the principle at work here is exactly the same as with the earlier Prairie fireplaces that stood at the heart of those Chicago homes from the early days of Wright's practice. What sets this house apart from those earlier homes, however, is the energy of the spatial freedom that the architect gains by abandoning the traditional geometry and the mainly solid walls. Wright built another house nearby and together they created a sensation.

V. C. MORRIS GIFT SHOP, SAN FRANCISCO, CALIFORNIA *1948*

Courtesy of the Frank Lloyd Wright Foundation

THE V. C. Morris Gift Shop in San Francisco is one of Frank Lloyd Wright's least well-known pieces, but it is nevertheless a most beautiful and accomplished design with some features that are worthy of note. Against all expectations, Wright created a plain brick façade, with the minimum of decoration, for this gift shop in San Francisco. At first glance, therefore, the building seems somewhat minimalist. On closer inspection, however, the building reveals typical Wrightian spatial cunning at work.

The entrance to the shop looks at first rather like a Romanesque arch but this is deceptive. In fact access to the shop is through only one half of the semi-circle; the other half, somewhat surprisingly, has been developed into a flower bed. The other external decorations are a light slot that runs from the beginning of the turn of the arch, and a row of light boxes at chest level that run from the flower bed across the rest of the front. The dynamic of this particular Frank Lloyd Wright building is really quite incredible: it looks plain, even old-fashioned, until the viewer realises the half-open, half-closed invitation to visit a space that looks private but is actually seeking visitors. Inside are ramps – the first Guggenheim plans date from this period – that draw shoppers up to look at the wares and to enjoy the openness of the internal space.

HOUSE FOR HERMAN T. MOSSBERG, SOUTH BEND, INDIANA *1948*

Courtesy of the Frank Lloyd Wright Foundation

THE floor plan of the House for Herman T. Mossberg is basically an L-shaped Usonian, but Wright came into conflict with the local planning authorities, who insisted that all domestic buildings should have two storeys.

Wright managed to get round these planning restrictions by creating a galleried second floor, with an upstairs bedroom for the Mossberg's daughter and an open mezzanine running down to a second-floor cavity, with storage above the workspace. The living room itself is two storeys high, with a monumental and cave-like fireplace offering a sense of shelter and warmth from one corner. There are two more bedrooms on the ground-floor level, beyond the mezzanined section. The planning authorities were satisfied. The inside of the L-shape is made of windowall, with glass from eaves to floor, allowing the entry of sunshine from the east and south.

HOUSE FOR CHARLES T. WELTZHEIMER, OBERLIN, OHIO *1948*

Courtesy of Alan Weintraub / Arcaid

THIS house was built on a lot that contained an apple orchard. Frank Lloyd Wright, as always taking his inspiration from nature and the immediate environment, used the idea of apples on a branch as the starting point for the abstract pattern in the clerestorey, rather as he had used the hollyhock as the inspiration for the decorative scheme for Aline Barnsdall's house of that name in California (see page 112).

Wright also asked all the members of the Weltzheimer family what in particular was it they wanted from their house, although the child who wanted a dog did not get the Wright-designed kennel that Eddie Berger enjoyed (see page 194). The Weltzheimer house was not built exactly as it was shown on the plans, and over the years many alterations were made that have gradually been undone. The future of the house is now secure, however: it has been offered as a gift to Oberlin College.

HOUSE FOR KENNETH LAURENT, ROCKFORD, ILLINOIS *1949*

Courtesy of William Allin Storrer (S.319)

KENNETH Laurent was a paraplegic, so Wright had to incorporate features into the house designed specifically to allow for wheelchair access, and he dispensed with any of the usual steps of a typical Usonian home.

Like the Jacobs house of 1944 (see page 166), the House for Kenneth Laurent is a solar hemicycle, although the grid is formed of 4-foot squares and the architect used a number of rectangular forms, for the main bedroom, the workspace and the utility–tool area. The private façade has a 'windowall' (a floor to ceiling wall of windows) with a pool and plants. The geometry is rather different from that of the House for Herbert Jacobs, however, where all the curves referred to one centre. In this house there are several centres, with overlapping circles of the same radius rather than circles of decreasing size. The house is built of brick, with Tidewater cypress trim, and the roof (since replaced) was made of tar and gravel.

HOUSE FOR WARD MCCARTNEY, PARKWYN VILLAGE, KALAMAZOO, MICHIGAN *1949*

Courtesy of William Allin Storrer (S.299)

PARKWYN Village was formed by a splinter group from the Galesburg County Homes project, which was the scheme of a group of people mostly employed by the Upjohn Company in Kalamazoo. The Parkwyn group felt that the Galesburg site was too far from Kalamazoo, where many of them worked. Wright designed many of the houses in the Parkwyn subdivision but only four were built.

This house, built of textile block made by Ward McCartney and Eric Brown, who was building one of the other Wright houses, is based on the 30/60 degree (right-angled) triangle, on a 4-foot diamond grid. It is a development of a one-room cottage that the architect had designed for his sister, with the living area in the larger triangle built first, and the smaller one added four months later, housing the quiet zone. The narrowest corner of the triangle was initially a bedroom but was turned into a study. The roof of the main section is a shallow pyramid that matches the proportions of the triangle ground plan, although the narrow end is cantilevered, giving the house both a ground-hugging and an aerodynamic appearance.

HOUSE FOR ROBERT BERGER, SAN ANSELMO, CALIFORNIA *1950*

Courtesy of Alan Weintraub/Arcaid

THE Bergers only had $15,000 to put into their house, so Wright designed them a simple Usonian in-line on a parellelogram grid. Robert Berger quarried and split the stone himself before putting it into place, also by hand, using a ladder and block and tackle. The plot of land that he and his wife were building on was in a magnificent situation on the hillside, and Wright's elevation fits snugly into the landscape so that, as he wished, the house seems to belong right there. Like the Ward McCartney house the Berger house was built in stages, with the master bedroom originally sited behind the workspace in one corner off the hexagonal living area, before the quiet zone was completed and the Bergers moved into the big room at the end of the gallery. Jim Berger, their son, was concerned that the family pooch, Eddie, had nowhere to live — Jim Berger therefore wrote to Frank Lloyd Wright requesting plans for a dog house, which were duly sent, with the result that a Wright-designed kennel is now attached to the outer wall of the shop, next to the carport.

HOUSE FOR RAYMOND CARLSON, PHOENIX, ARIZONA 1950

Courtesy of Alan Weintraub / Arcaid

WRIGHT used a different construction system for this very beautiful house, which he liked so much that he included it in his book on the Usonians, *The Natural House* (1954). It is built from wooden posts, enamel-painted to protect them from the heat, and cement asbestos panels – a technique that goes right back to the board-and-batten houses of his Oak Park practice (see Summer Cottage for E. H. Pitkin page 32). The difference here is that the architect used the wooden posts both vertically and horizontally – not only as supports in the wall but also as beams in the roof. The structure uses half levels in a visually pleasing way: the entrance, from ground level, leads directly into the living room, with the workspace and dining room at the other end half a level down, and the bedrooms half a level up. Above them are the roof garden and the penthouse study. The Carlsons were good friends with the Wrights – the architect sent them a piano as a gift after the party to celebrate the building's completion, a piano costing more than his fee.

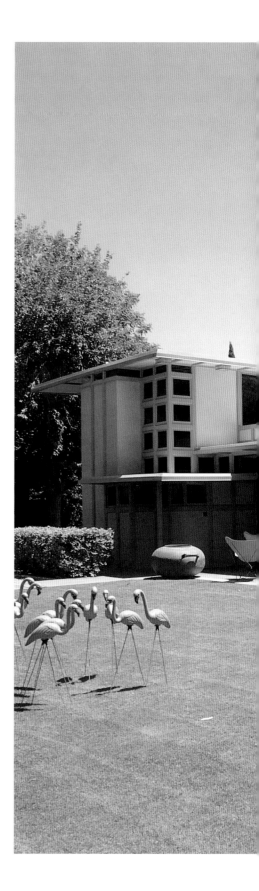

HOUSE FOR SEAMOUR SHAVIN, CHATTANOOGA, TENNESSEE *1950*

Courtesy of William Allin Storrer (S.339)

THIS, an in-line (all the rooms in a row) Usonian house, is the only building that Frank Lloyd Wright designed in the state of Tennessee. It is located on a ridge, just below the summit, so that it belongs very much to the ground but is nevertheless high enough for its inhabitants to be able to see over the neighbours towards a view of the Tennessee river and the nearby mountains.

This house has a dramatically sloping roof over the living room: this is known as a 'butterfly' roof and is one of the many variations on a flat or hipped roof that the architect used in the Usonians. The house is built of stone brought from a local quarry and assembled unevenly so that the shapes of the different pieces appear on the wall's surface, and of red Tidewater cypress, another local material. The masonry is similar in effect to the walls at Taliesin and very characteristic of Wright's work. The quiet zone of the house is half a level lower than the living zone because the ground slopes away.

HOUSE FOR DAVID WRIGHT AND GUEST HOUSE, PHOENIX, ARIZONA *1954*

Courtesy of the Frank Lloyd Wright Foundation

AS in the designs for Florida Southern College (see pages 148–153), Wright here used the idea of citrus foliage as a replacement lawn for houses in the desert. David Wright was the architect's fourth son, and he worked in the concrete-block industry. However, when his father produced plans for a house built out of a different material they had to be reworked so that his home could be built from the blocks he promoted. William Wesley Peters, the architect's son-in-law and a key colleague, undertook the redrafting.

The house is built on a circular plan, with 10-degree slices of circle as the basic unit. Concrete pillars raise the house to a height from which it can 'sit' on the citrus foliage, and this raised level is reached via a ramp that continues the curvature of the circle. All of the accommodation, both living and sleeping, is on the main floor, and on the inside of the circle the architect specified a garden court, complete with an almond-shaped pool, which can be seen from all the rooms.

HOUSE FOR NATHAN AND JEANNE RUBIN 1951

Courtesy of Alan Weintraub / Arcaid

THE plan of this house mirrors one of the designs that the architect undertook for the first Usonian project in Okemos, of which only the Goetsch–Winkler house (see page 158) was built. Wright did sometimes reuse plans where the needs of more than one client coincided, and/or where the topography was similar. The basic materials are a mixture of brick and redwood, and as always Wright planned the house to give its owners privacy – defeated on this occasion by the subsequent re-routing of the nearby road.

The floorplan here is on a 2-foot by 4-foot rectangular grid, with the quiet zone set on a line with three bedrooms and two bathrooms. The architect set a second axis of the house at 120 degrees to this, with a 32-foot hexagon holding the living and work spaces next to the end of the quiet zone. The fireplace is just off the centre of the hexagon, set aside to allow room for the dining area to be located next to the workspace. Jeanne Rubin was a teacher who had an abiding interest in crystallography, a science related to the Froebel gifts that had had such an influence on Wright as a child and a young man.

HOUSE FOR DR RICHARD DAVIS, MARION, INDIANA *1951*

Courtesy of the Frank Lloyd Wright Foundation

WRIGHT'S lifelong preoccupation with the idea of an architecture indigenous to America, not derived from the ancient classical aesthetics that came from Europe, led him inevitably to consider the teepee as a form. He first made use of it in plans for a colony beside Lake Tahoe, but the stock market crash of 1929 spelt the end for that scheme. However, good ideas are never lost – only recycled in a new form. After the Second World War Wright reconsidered the idea of a one-room house, partitioned to reflect the different uses its inhabitants would make of the interior space: the McCartney house (see page 192) is an example of this idiom.

The central octagonal teepee section is 38-feet high, with a masonry core containing the fireplace and chimney, and sits right in the middle, reflecting the style of its Native American predecessors. Wright then created a bedroom wing running south-west from the central section. Another was added to the north after his death, complete with a hurricane shelter in the basement.

ANDERTON COURT SHOPS, BEVERLY HILLS, CALIFORNIA *1952*

Courtesy of the Frank Lloyd Wright Foundation

THIS mini-mall of shops that Wright created on Rodeo Drive in downtown Beverly Hills is geometrically unexpected, consisting of white shapes that together form a pattern set on a diamond-shaped grid. It presents a bright and dramatic vista to the shopper driving towards the mall. Wright was originally commissioned to design four shops for the mall, but the scheme was later expanded to include an additional one.

The Anderton Court Shops complex is certainly an interesting and unusual space to be in, as the whiteness of the concrete, combined with the blue Californian sky, make the angular composition, softened with circular windows, seem intriguing and spatially complex. On the summit of the building is a striking decorative spike, whose pattern evokes the shapes used by the South American Indians whose work had inspired Wright in previous commissions, such as the Hollyhock House (see page 112). In order to reach the different shops in the mall the visitor must climb up a hexagonal ramp. On the ramp the visitor can enjoy vistas into the different elements of the building. Although the geometry is inviting, the overall complex does not in fact have a particularly restful atmosphere and it lacks the organic attachment to its surroundings that is such an attractive feature of Frank Lloyd Wright's work.

HOUSE FOR QUENTIN BLAIR, CODY, WYOMING *1952*

Courtesy of Alan Weintraub / Arcaid

THIS beautiful sandstone and Philippine mahogany Usonian house sits on the plain in Wyoming not far from the beautiful Yellowstone National Park. It is Frank Lloyd Wright's only building in this state. The town of Cody is famous as the home of Buffalo Bill, and Quentin Blair owned the Buffalo Bill Village nearby.

For the house that Quentin Blair commissioned Wright to build the architect decided to set the local stone into the wall in varied positions so that its character as a material is easy to see. He also varied the square grid by setting the workspace at 45 degrees to the living room, with a triangular niche for the piano suggesting the other corner. This means that living room is not in fact a simple shape but has its own angular energy created by the inventive use of angles and the positioning of furniture. The roof soars upwards as it does in the Seamour Shavin house (see page 198), giving a view across the plain to the distant horizon.

HOUSE FOR RAY BRANDES, ISSAQUAH, WASHINGTON *1952*

Courtesy of Alan Weintraub/Arcaid

THIS house for Ray Brandes is almost a mirror-image of the house that Wright created for Alma Goetsch and Katherine Winkler (see page 156), on the same 4-foot-square module. It is built out of concrete textile block, the material that Wright had championed since the 1920s (see House for John Storer page 116).

Another of Wright's trademarks to appear in this house is the clerestory, a great favourite of Wrights and one which he used to great effect to ensure that light penetrated the innermost spaces of his houses. A clerestory is made by raising a part of the roof and putting glass between the lower and upper levels so that sunlight make its way in not just from the outer walls of the house but also from its very heart. And because the clerestorey offered this inner light, the architect often decorated it with patterns that enhanced the geometric harmony of the living space: here, however, it is designed only to let in as much light as possible.

PRICE TOWER FOR THE H. C. PRICE COMPANY, BARTLESVILLE, OKLAHOMA 1952

Courtesy of the Frank Lloyd Wright Foundation

FOR the Romeo and Juliet windmill tower (see page 24) Wright used a central 'tap root' foundation to support its structure and Wright himself said that this little building was of great help to him in later years as he created unique, beautiful and spatially exquisite towers. He believed that the tower should stand alone in the prairie like a tree escaped from the forest, and not be surrounded by other blocks. In this unusual, functional and supremely elegant tower he achieved his goal. Its design was influenced by the plans that he drew for a tower in New York for St Mark's in the Bouwerie, where the central core carried all the utilities and the floors are cantilevered out from it in the same way as they are in the Johnson Wax Research Tower.

The Price Tower is nineteen floors high, and is composed of four segments that are pinwheeled around the central core of the building. Three of these four segments are single-storey office spaces, and the fourth houses eight duplex apartments. Wright himself has one floor as living space, with two bedrooms galleried above. The office façades are primarily horizontal, with alternate gold and green copper bands, whereas the apartments have a vertical emphasis because of the long slender mullions. The windows are easy to open. Wright managed to successfully design a tower that was open and inviting and which does not suffer from the hermetically sealed detachment from human and natural life that is so often a characteristic of tower blocks.

COTTAGE FOR JORGINE BOOMER, PHOENIX, ARIZONA 1953

Courtesy of Alan Weintraub/Arcaid

JORGINE Boomer was a member of the Dupont family, and she commissioned Frank Lloyd Wright to create this glorious, pointed, energetic house in Phoenix, Arizona, which shoots dynamically up from its desert surroundings.

The Cottage for Jorgine Boomer is built, appropriately for its setting, from desert masonry construction. The two-dimensional geometry is the 60/120-degree parallelogram, with the larger mass holding the living space and a smaller, triangular carport and chauffeur's dwelling growing off it. The chimney is set right at the heart of the house, offering the central masonry support, and there are fireplaces in both the living room and the main bedroom. The third dimension arrives from the pointing, light-enhancing roof. It is this roof which makes the space inside seem to flow from the hot open spaces of the desert without: a development from the angled but rectangular roof of earlier buildings.

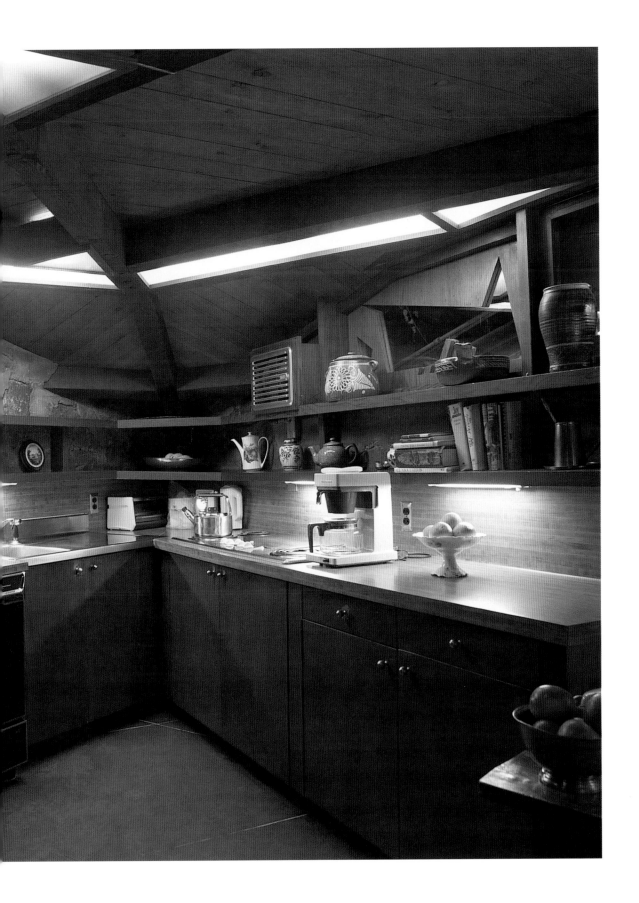

HOUSE FOR JOHN DOBKINS, CANTON, OHIO *1953*

Courtesy of Alan Weintraub / Arcaid

THE House for John Dobkins in Ohio is another example of a house that is perfectly integrated into its environment.

The visitor approaching the Dobkins house has really no clue to the unusual site that awaits from the garden façade, where the one-and-a-half-storey living room is walled in glass, and the ceiling slopes downwards in a cosy, earth-hugging embrace. The result is quite different from the dramatic sloping roof of House for Jack Lamberson (see page 182). With the Lamberson house the visual effect is of light, flight and movement. Here, however, the house seems to really love its wooded landscape setting and to be intimately attached to it, while the greenery outside is integral to the interior because of the sheer extent of glass used in the construction.

Unusually for Wright he cut corners with cost on this house: the roof was enamel painted blue-green, which gave the effect of copper but cost considerably less.

HOUSE FOR CEDRIC BOULTER, CINCINNATI, OHIO *1954*

Courtesy of Alan Weintraub/Arcaid

THE house that Wright created for Cedric Boulter is built into the side of a slope. This means that although the public façade looks as though it has only a single storey, in fact the house opens downwards to take advantage of the landscape in which it is situated.

Just as with the second house for Herbert Jacobs (see page 166) and Wright's other solar hemicycle houses, the quiet zone is galleried, although the plan is in-line and not curved. Here the balcony is suspended from the roof, as are the stairs that lead upwards from the entrance to the galleried area. The upper floor of the house extends beyond the outside wall in a cantilevered extension to form an external raised terrace. Concrete block and Douglas fir are the main structural materials that Wright used here, with Philippine mahogany trim, African mahogany stairs and Taliesin red concrete floors, on which the four-foot square unit of the floor plan is clearly marked.

Beth Sholom Synagogue, Elkins Park, Pennsylvania *1954*

Courtesy of the Frank Lloyd Wright Foundation

EACH of Wright's designs for places of worship, from Unity Temple (see page 56) onwards, expresses his sense of the divine present in the congregation, gathered in a building designed for its use. In this great synagogue he took advice from a range of scholars who understood Jewish symbolism; indeed, the congregation's rabbi, Mortimer J. Cohen, is credited with the architect on the designs.

Wright's brief was to include in the building visual references to both American and Jewish forms. The great blue plastic pyramid that stands over the 1,000-seat auditorium can be seen as either a tent or a mountain: the holy Mount Sinai, on which God gave Moses the ten commandments. The Torah (the holy books) is seen as the source of light; at night the pyramid glows from within like a beacon. The sanctuary roof is supported by a steel frame, with each of the major beams measuring over 35 metres in length; this means that the pyramid needs no other internal support. Members of the congregation speak as warmly of this building as do the Unitarians who worship at Unity Temple.

HOUSE FOR ELLIS FEIMAN, CANTON, OHIO *1954*

Courtesy of Alan Weintraub / Arcaid

MRS Feiman was the sister of Jeanne Rubin (see House for Nathan and Jeanne Rubin page 202). The house that Wright designed for the Feimans derived from the 1953 New York Usonian Exhibition House, assembled on the site that would later hold the Guggenheim museum, as a part of the exhibition 'Sixty Years of Living Architecture: The Work of Frank Lloyd Wright'. This exhibition opened at the Palazzo Strozzi and toured Europe before coming to New York.

Unlike the exhibition house, which was built out of pipe scaffolding covered with wire glass and cement and asbestos boards, the Feiman house is built of brick with wood trim. The house has a taller than usual clerestory, patterned on the public façade with a geometric motif of lines and squares. Wright was still trying to meet the challenge of providing low-cost housing for the mass of American people but in reality these houses still cost more than most could afford.

HOUSE FOR I. N. HAGAN, CHALKHILL, PENNSYLVANIA 1954

Courtesy of Alan Weintraub/Arcaid

THIS house for I. N. Hagan is one of Wright's most successful integrations of a building with its landscape.

As so often with Wright's buildings, the house is a situated just below the summit of its hill, the Kentuck Knob, which is one of the higher peaks in the Western Pennsylvania Highlands. It is built of split but unpolished sandstone, which has weathered over the years to a calm grey colour similar to that of the wood, red Tidewater cypress, after the elements have aged and quietened it. The roof is copper. The views from the house are spectacular; Wright designed the living room so that one end is sharply angled, seeming to press forward from the house – in the winter like the prow of a iceship through its element. Hexagon/triangle/diamond geometry, and 60/120 degree-angles govern throughout, although they are not evident from the floor, which is covered in various materials – cork tile in the workspace, stone in the living room and carpet elsewhere.

Grandma House for Harold Price, Paradise Valley, Arizona *1954*

Courtesy of Alan Weintraub / Arcaid

HAROLD Price Sr was a very good patron of Wright's: he and his son commissioned the Price Tower (see page 212) as well as this and another domestic residence. This house was designed as a retirement home for the parents, and, unlike some of the works that emerged from his studio in the 1950s, Wright took a great personal interest in the details of this building.

At the heart of the Grandma House for Harold Price is an open-air atrium, which is walled by concrete posts and wood. The roof sits above the space on elegant steel pillars that rise from the concrete to give a structure over a clerestory that is open to desert breezes while still offering shelter. In the centre of the atrium is a fountain, above which is a skylight, so that light and water together offer constant movement. The roof's edges are decorated with punched copper that throws more broken shadows, a play of light that seems appropriate for the broken desert terrain.

HOUSE FOR GERALD TONKENS, CINCINNATI, OHIO *1954*

Courtesy of Alan Weintraub/Arcaid

RIGHT up until the end of his life, Frank Lloyd Wright continued to try to resolve the enigma of creating housing that was both cheap and beautiful, so that everyone could have access to a good space for living at a price they could afford. This theme, which was one that the architect wrestled with continually, was first articulated in the concept of Broadacre City (see page 132), and it runs through much of his work. The idea of a Usonian Automatic house was just one further development along these lines.

The idea of the Usonian Automatic was that as much of it should be prefabricated as was possible, in order that it could be built simply, even by the clients themselves. Wright designed seven variations on the theme, of which this House for Gerald Tonkens is the last. The house is built of concrete block, pierced concrete block (that is, concrete framing glass) and glass. However, this was not a cheap house: it took seventeen months to construct and was sited in a 6-acre lot.

DALLAS THEATER CENTER FOR PAUL BAKER, DALLAS, TEXAS *1955*

Courtesy of the Frank Lloyd Wright Foundation

THE Kalita Humphreys Theater, which is part of the Dallas Theater Center, was greeted with an enormous amount of enthusiasm on its construction: one critic described it as 'in itself justifying a visit to this city'.

The theater's revolving stage is divided into three sections for ease of set manoeuvring. This means that one scene can be on stage, another can be under construction and the other being struck (dismantled) all at the same time. The stage drum rises above the cantilevered masses of concrete to give a lightness to what is otherwise a massive and monumental construction, although the interior space is serene and extremely effective for its purpose. Over 400 people can be seated in the theater's auditorium, in just 11 rows. The rows wrap around the stage in three sides of a hexagon and this allows for an intimate performance, with the audience situated close to the stage, but without experiencing a sense of crowding, which is good for the actors too.

HOUSE FOR RANDALL FAWCETT, LOS BANOS, CALIFORNIA *1955*

Courtesy of Alan Weintraub/Arcaid

THE Fawcetts were a family who farmed a part of the central valley of California, and their house in Los Banos is surrounded by a green canopy of walnut trees. Constructed of concrete block, the front entrance, as is so often the case with Wright's buildings, is highly deceptive and gives little clue to the considerable spaces of the interior of the house. In fact, all that can be seen from the outside of the building is a part of the clerestorey in the living room alcove, which is a partial hexagon next to the hearth.

The living room is located right at the centre of the house. The living room has a huge fireplace with a high cantilevered mantel in the back wall: two wings lead away from the ends of the room, set at 60 degrees to it. The basic unit of the House for Randall Fawcett is the equilateral triangle. One of the wings contains a playroom, and at the end of the playroom is a swimming pool, also shaped on the grid.

HOUSE FOR MAX HOFFMAN, RYE, NEW YORK *1955*

Courtesy of Alan Weintraub/Arcaid

THE house that Frank Lloyd Wright created for Max Hoffman is particularly notable for the beauty of its materials and for the great care that was taken in its construction: all the wood was specially selected so that it matched for grain at all the joints, both horizontal and vertical. The stone was hand chipped and, as was Wright's practice in so many of his domestic designs, the horizontal mortar was deeply raked while that in the vertical joins was left flush with the surface.

The architect chose flagstones for the floor, so the usual definition of the underlying unit is missing, except where it is shown by the windows or by built-in furniture. The gallery that runs along the courtyard side of the house has an abstract-patterned clerestorey that seems to suggest speed, energy and the grill of a racing car: Max Hoffman worked as an importer and seller of Mercedes Benz automobiles, and Wright also designed his car showroom in New York City.

KUNDERT MEDICAL CLINIC, SAN LUIS OBISPO, CALIFORNIA *1955*

Courtesy of Alan Weintraub / Arcaid

THIS eye clinic that Wright created for Drs Kundert and Fogo has an L-shaped Usonian floorplan (see House for Herbert Jacobs page 136), which was modified to suit the special needs of a clinic rather than a home. The waiting room takes the space of the living room, and at the end of each wing there is a room without windows for the special testing and visual analysis that the ophthalmologists needed to undertake.

The waiting room of the clinic has a triple clerestory – that is three layers of the usual narrow windows – with an abstract decorative pattern on it. This arrangement brings a shapely and unexpected light and shadow to the space within. The abstract pattern evokes both mountains and waves, movement and monumentality, and must certainly have made the waiting room an extremely interesting space for patients to sit in while waiting to see their optician.

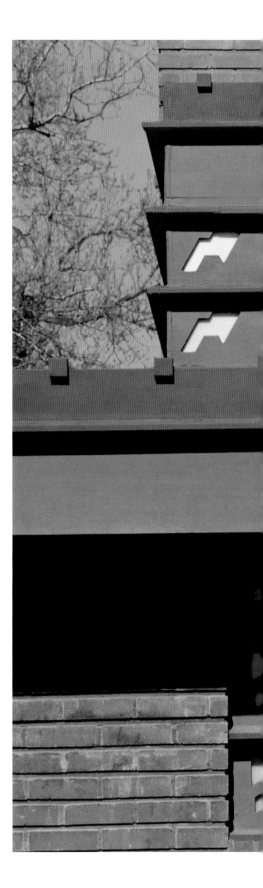

THE ERDMAN PREFABS, WISCONSIN AND ILLINOIS *1956–57*

Courtesy of the Frank Lloyd Wright Foundation

WRIGHT'S last contribution to the continuing development of housing for the wider market – although in truth even these were beyond the income of the average family – were the so-called Erdman Prefabs, which developed from the idea of the Usonian Automatic (see House for Gerald Tonkens page 228). These were a range of three prefabricated models that he created to be manufactured by Marshall Erdman Associates, a Madison Wisconsin building firm; only two designs were actually constructed. The core of the houses was built out of masonry on a concrete slab floor, with painted exterior panel siding made of Masonite board and interior mahogany plywood.

One of the clients for the Erdman prefabs was a medic named Dr Arnold Jackson who stitched up Wright's nose after he got into a fight at Halloween in 1932; he and his wife became firm friends with the architect. Another client earned his living putting up telegraph poles. When he and his wife visited Taliesin to meet their architect they passed through his office on their way out, bored by waiting for him to pass by – they said they had not expected to meet him, and he replied (aged ninety-one), 'Young man, you're very lucky'.

SOLOMON R. GUGGENHEIM MUSEUM, NEW YORK *1956*

Courtesy of Richard Bryant/Arcaid

THIS, one of Wright's most famous, popular and attractive works, was also one of the longest in creation. He began work on a 'temple of non-objectivity' in 1943. Despite the opposition of the New York zoning authorities and some (perhaps fortunate) limitations on budget – one draft scheme has the building clad in bright pink marble – the building was opened in December 1959. The result is a building both entirely suited to its purpose and a supreme artistic, plastic and sculptural achievement – a familiar New York landmark from the outside and a joy for art lovers and visitors within.

Perhaps the most significant feature of the building is the ramp, which is reminiscent of the V. C. Morris Gift Shop in San Francisco (see page 184), running upwards around a spiral of increasing diameter at a very gentle gradient. Visitors are swept upwards in a lift to descend from the skylight, whose beams are extensions of the discreet structural pillars on the outer walls, to wander slowly down, enjoying the space as well as the art displayed. They can see the pictures either intimately or with a broader perspective, across the gallery to the opposite ramp, in a spatial freedom that is unique and quintessentially Wrightian.

CLINIC FOR DR KENNETH MEYERS, DAYTON, OHIO *1956*

Courtesy of Alan Weintraub/Arcaid

IN this building for Dr Kenneth Meyers Wright came up with a typically quirky but geometrically satisfying answer to the question of how to arrange a medical clinic.

The patient arrives through an entry between two rectangles, which are set together not at a right angle but at a wider, right-angle-and-a-half: on the left is the waiting room, a harmonious and regular rectangular space. When called to see the doctor, however, the patient moves into a more mobile zone – also rectangular but with half an octagon joined to it to supply examination rooms. The laboratory is situated under the peak of the octagon, with the practice library tucked away on the far side. The opposite side of the rectangle contains further examination rooms and the x-ray space, with a darkroom attached. This means that the surgery area, unlike the waiting room, itself invites change and a sense of progression – architectural optimism appropriate for a centre of healing.

WYOMING VALLEY SCHOOL, WYOMING VALLEY, WISCONSIN *1956*

Courtesy of the Frank Lloyd Wright Foundation

THIS is the only public (that is, state) elementary school building designed by Wright – in fact, designed for free and partly paid for by him as well, since the governors said they could not afford his fee. The building part of his contribution was a memorial to his mother. It is a lovely, low-slung, horizontal and peaceful construction, with windows all around, made up of two large classrooms and an assembly room/cafeteria, all, of course, around a central fireplace. The overall visual effect of the house is reminiscent of some of the Prairie buildings (see House for Arthur Heurtley, page 44), with overhanging eaves, a sense of the building hugging both the ground and the central block of the chimney. Inside, the openness of the space and its articulation in triangles and hexagons belong clearly to the latter stages of Wright's long and prolific creativity. The school resembles the building that he thought of in the Broadacre City plans, so the mission was still continuing.

ANNUNCIATION GREEK ORTHODOX CHURCH, WAUWATOSA, WISCONSIN *1957*

Courtesy of the Frank Lloyd Wright Foundation

THIS extraordinary church, which looks on first acquaintance a bit like a flying saucer, is in fact based on pure geometry relating to great buildings of both the Renaissance and Graeco-Roman times. The traditional Greek cross is inscribed within a circle, and the cross itself is composed of segments of the circle but turned inside out. The roof is gently convex while the part-circles that shape the cross are concave, giving a sense of balance and serenity that belongs to the Orthodox tradition of symmetrical and harmonious churches. Lighting comes not from the blue roof but from coloured glass windows around the perimeter of the building. On the outside wall, each arm of the inner cruciform is decorated with a cross. On the ground floor a banqueting hall and Sunday school classrooms extend out from the main circle. A sunken garden surrounds the whole building. Within the sanctuary, the congregation sits in the centre of the circle and in three of the arms, the fourth being the chancel and altar. On the first level a circular balcony offers more seating than the whole ground level. It is interesting to see that there are still numerous visual connections between this circular space for worship and the cuboid Unity Temple (see page 56).

HOUSE FOR JOHN RAYWARD, NEW CANAAN, CONNECTICUT, PLAYHOUSE FOR VICTORIA *1957, additions 1958*

Courtesy of the Frank Lloyd Wright Foundation

THIS house was called Tirranna, an aboriginal word meaning 'running waters' – it is set close to the Noroton river and is surrounded by running water. The gardens and woodland are notable in themselves, and the whole site is remarkable for its beauty and individuality.

The building is unusual among the architect's work for its combination of a hemispherical main living area and an L-shaped quiet zone – the latter is also remarkable for the observatory that was built for John Rayward above the main bedroom's adjacent dressing room. All of the house's furniture, fabric and carpet was designed by Wright. Like the Ward McCartney house (see page 192), this was built in sections.

In addition to the main building the architect created a playhouse for the Rayward's daughters, Victoria and Jennifer, another hemispheric structure whose rooftop terrace overlooks the stream that flows into the pond and waterway around the house itself. Fish steps were built so that aquatic life could climb up against the current as well as flowing down with the stream.

MARIN COUNTY CIVIC CENTER AND POST OFFICE, SAN RAFAEL, CALIFORNIA *1957*

Courtesy of Alan Weintraub/Arcaid

THE Civic Center, comprising the Hall of Justice and the Administration Building, is one of the very few state-sponsored buildings designed by Wright, and the San Rafael Post Office is the only government building of his. Both embody many of the principles that he had long espoused and had articulated in Broadacre City (see page 132). The Civic Center seems ideal for its site, stretching in two long curves towards the hills, embracing the ground and without the vertical assertiveness of other, more explicitly authoritative buildings of state. Wright clearly expresses the primacy of the happy citizen: the main entrance is an outdoor terrace with water features (a pool and fountain) and a garden, and beneath the dome beyond is a library. The centre arches over the highway, joining its life to the flow of the people it was designed to serve. The geometry is circular, with arches rising in layers reminiscent, from some angles, of Roman aqueducts – the classical purity is unsurprising and the reference grows from Wright's grasp of the fundamental principles of harmony rather than from some pale imitation.

HOUSE FOR DON STROMQUIST, BOUNTIFUL, UTAH *1958*

Courtesy of Alan Weintraub / Arcaid

THIS House for Don Stromquist is the only building that Frank Lloyd Wright created in the state of Utah. It is built on a diamond grid and is constructed out of concrete block and mahogany trim. The bedrooms are clustered around the back of the workspace, each with a 120-degree angle as its external corner, and this gives them a very open and spacious feeling.

The fireplace in the living room continues this dynamic, facing prow-like towards the Wright-designed table, which is itself set at 120 degrees to the wall. Wright also specified benches all around the room, beneath the windows whose 120-degree corners are mitred (the glass is invisibly joined). The carving detail on the shutters is a particularly beautiful feature of this house, and is reminiscent of the clerestory detail in the Kundert Medical Clinic (see page 236). The building is oriented in order to take best advantage of the sunsets in the surrounding valley.

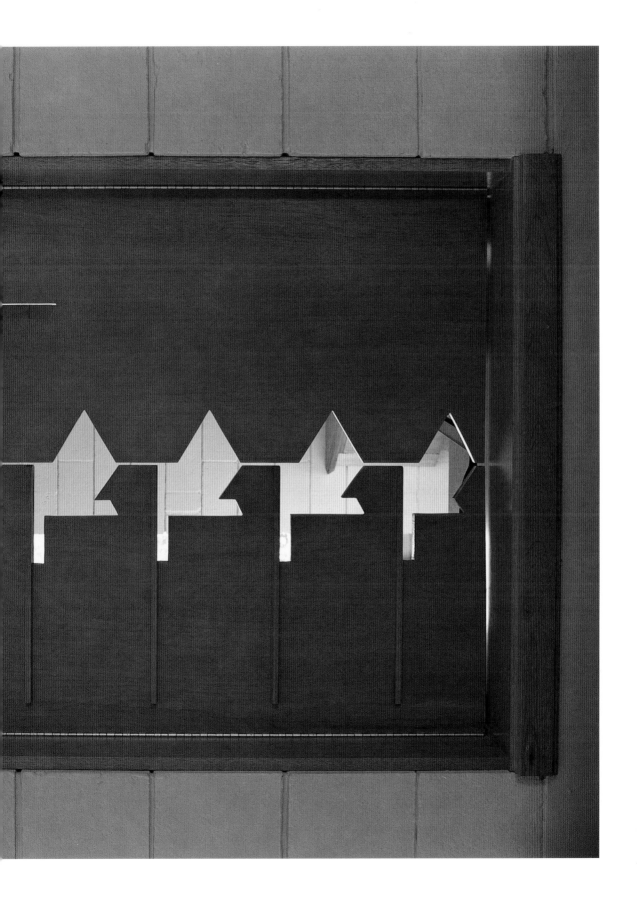

HOUSE FOR NORMAN LYKES, PHOENIX, ARIZONA *1959*

Courtesy of the Frank Lloyd Wright Foundation

THIS is the last design by Wright to be built by the original client, although one of the Taliesin architects (John Rattenbury) is the architect of record. Wright made sketches and Rattenbury drew up plans from these, much as John H. Howe did on many other buildings in the later years of the Taliesin Fellowship.

This building is made up of circles, from the garden court to the workspace to the living room, and even the quiet zone is built on an arc. The house stands on a desert slope, surrounded by stone, cacti and scrub, and it peaks above its surroundings like a space-age intruder – there is some similarity here with the Greek Orthodox Church at Wauwatosa (see page 246). The material was concrete block, tinted the colour of desert roses, and mahogany trim; it must have been an intriguing building to live in, even if it does not have the sureness of touch of some of the earlier Usonians.

FURTHER READING

Frank Lloyd Wright *An Autobiography* (Duell, Sloan and Pierce, 1932 and 1967).

Frank Lloyd Wright *The Japanese Print: An interpretation* (Horizon, 1967).

McCarter, Robert *Frank Lloyd Wright* (Phaidon Press, 1997).

Storrer, William Allin *Frank Lloyd Wright Companion*
(University of Chicago Press, 1993).

Twombly, Robert C. *Frank Lloyd Wright: His Life and His Architecture*
(John Wiley & Sons, Inc., 1979).

There is a great deal of good material about the architect on the Internet. The Frank Lloyd Wright Organization website is as good a place as any to start (http://www.franklloydwright.org/index.html).